University Success

READING AND WRITING

HIGH-BEGINNING

Carrie Steenburgh

University Success Reading and Writing, High-Beginning

Copyright © 2020 by Pearson Education, Inc.

All rights reserved.

Pearson Education, 221 River Street, Hoboken, NJ 07030

Staff credits: The people who made up the *University Success* team, representing content development, design, manufacturing, marketing, multimedia, project management, publishing, rights management, and testing, are Pietro Alongi, Sheila Ameri, Stephanie Callahan, Tracey Cataldo, Dave Dickey, Gina DiLillo, Warren Fischbach, Nancy Flaggman, Sarah Henrich, Niki Lee, Agnieszka Leszkiewicz, Amy McCormick, Robert Ruvo, Katarzyna Starzynska-Kosciuszko, Paula Van Ells, and Joseph Vella.

Project management: Debbie Sistino

Instructional design: Tim McLaughlin

Contributing editors: Eleanor Kirby Barnes, Linda Butler, Jaimie Scanlon, Leigh Stolle, and Sarah Wales-McGrath

Video production: Daniel Chávez-Ontiveros, Erendira Olivera, and *Think Films*

Video coordination: Robyn Brinks Lockwood

Video research: Constance Rylance

Text composition: EMC Design Ltd

Library of Congress Cataloging-in-Publication Data

A catalog record for the print edition is available from the Library of Congress.

Printed in the United States of America

ISBN-10: 0-13-524593-1

ISBN-13: 978-0-13-524593-4

8 2022

Contents

Welcome to *University Success*

INTRODUCTION

University Success is a five-level academic series designed to equip beginning through transition level English learners with the language skills necessary to succeed in university courses. At the upper levels, the three strands, Reading, Writing, and Oral Communication, are fully aligned across content and skills and provide students with an inspiring collection of extensive authentic content. The series has been developed in cooperation with subject matter experts, all thought leaders in their fields. The upper levels are organized around five distinct content areas—The Human Experience, Money and Commerce, The Science of Nature, Arts and Letters, and Structural Science. By focusing on STEAM topics, *University Success* helps equip students with the critical thinking skills and creative innovation necessary for success in their future careers.

University Success levels from Intermediate to Transition model the type of real-life learning situations that students face when studying for a degree. The lower levels, Beginning and High-Beginning, lay the groundwork and build the support that students need to prepare them for the complexity and challenge of the upper levels.

BUILDING THE FOUNDATION

Beginning students face a daunting challenge as they build the English-language skills needed for academic success. The Beginning and High-Beginning levels support these students by providing the scaffolding to construct a strong linguistic core. The two integrated skills strands (Reading and Writing and Listening and Speaking) include four distinct content areas that link to the content areas of the *University Success* upper levels. This allows students to build a background in basic concepts and vocabulary in these STEAM content areas: Business, Humanities, Structural Science, and Natural Science. These levels fuse high-interest, engaging content with carefully scaffolded tasks to develop the language skills needed for managing complex and conceptually challenging content.

Task types are recycled across content areas to reinforce skills and give students the confidence they need to take on ever-more challenging material. By using Bloom's Taxonomy as a framework, *University Success* strongly emphasizes the learning process. The series's targeted approach to vocabulary instruction includes both academic and high-frequency vocabulary and provides the basic building blocks needed to construct meaningful speech and writing. A variety of level-appropriate input, as well as visuals, organizers, and critical thinking and discussion activities enable students to fully internalize the content and solidify their linguistic foundation.

TWO STRANDS SUPPORT THE PATH TO LEARNER AUTONOMY

The two lower-level strands are fully aligned across content areas and skills, allowing teachers to utilize material from different strands to support learning. The strands are complementary, providing the teacher with aligned content across all four skills to be utilized in an integrated skills classroom. This allows students to build a solid background in basic concepts and vocabulary in each of the four content areas.

BEGINNING LEVEL

CEFR **A1**   GSE **22–32**

READING AND WRITING

Architecture

Genetics

Business and Technology

Psychology

SKILLS

- Identify the main idea
- Understand compare and contrast
- Express likes and preferences
- Write basic descriptions
- Write basic directions

LISTENING AND SPEAKING

Architecture

Genetics

Business and Technology

Psychology

SKILLS

- Understand the gist
- Identify compare and contrast signposts
- Express likes and preferences
- Describe people, places, and things
- Give basic instructions

HIGH-BEGINNING LEVEL

CEFR **A2–A2+**   GSE **33–42**

READING AND WRITING

Money and E-Commerce

Cultural Anthropology

Civil Engineering

Sustainable Agriculture

SKILLS

- Preview and predict
- Scan for details
- Recognize narratives
- Follow steps in a process
- Write a simple story
- Describe visuals

LISTENING AND SPEAKING

Money and E-Commerce

Cultural Anthropology

Civil Engineering

Sustainable Agriculture

SKILLS

- Predict
- Listen for details
- Identify events in a narrative
- Understand steps in a process
- Tell a story
- Describe objects

BUILDING THE FOUNDATION FOR *UNIVERSITY SUCCESS*

Two integrated-skills strands with explicit skill development tied to specific learning outcomes establish the foundation for higher-level academic success.

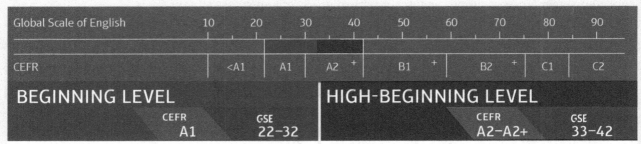

BEGINNING LEVEL
CEFR A1 **GSE** 22–32

The Beginning level gives students the fundamental building blocks and confidence to take on academic challenges.

INTENSIVE SKILL PRACTICE

Intensive skill practice tied to learning objectives informed by the Global Scale of English

ACADEMIC HIGH-INTEREST CONTENT

- Academic content linked to STEAM disciplines provides a bridge to the upper levels.
- Introducing each unit is a video featuring an overview of the academic area.
- High-interest topics and a variety of genres increase motivation.
- Two chapters within each content unit include recycled tasks and vocabulary and give students a solid background in basic concepts.

SCAFFOLDED APPROACH

- Chapters are heavily scaffolded with multiple guided exercises that follow Bloom's Taxonomy as a framework.
- Prediction and skill comprehension tasks accompany each reading and listening.
- Step-by-step application of all productive skills is practiced throughout each chapter.
- Readings and listenings are "chunked" and include accompanying visuals.
- Extensive integration of graphic organizers is included.

EXPLICIT VOCABULARY INSTRUCTION

A targeted approach to vocabulary including
- contextualized previews with pronunciation practice
- reviews in the Student Book and in MyEnglishLab
- collaborative tasks
- vocabulary tips
- a vocabulary building and expansion section
- an end-of-chapter vocabulary checklist

GRAMMAR FOR WRITING / SPEAKING

A dedicated grammar presentation with controlled practice tasks in the Student Book and in MyEnglishLab provide scaffolding for the writing and speaking tasks.

SOFT SKILLS

Task-based strategies linked to chapter topics focus on academic success, life skills, and college readiness.

HIGH-BEGINNING LEVEL
CEFR A2–A2+ **GSE** 33–42

The High-Beginning level builds the support that prepares students for the rigor and challenges of the upper levels and beyond.

INTENSIVE SKILL PRACTICE

Intensive skill practice tied to learning objectives informed by the Global Scale of English

ACADEMIC HIGH-INTEREST CONTENT

- Academic content linked to STEAM disciplines provides a bridge to the upper levels.
- Introducing each unit is a video featuring a university professor, which gives students an academic perspective.
- High-interest topics and a variety of genres increase motivation.
- Two chapters within each content unit include recycled tasks and vocabulary and give students a solid background in academic concepts.

SCAFFOLDED APPROACH

- Chapters are carefully scaffolded with multiple guided exercises that follow Bloom's Taxonomy as a framework.
- Practical application of all productive skills is integrated in every chapter.
- Readings and listenings are "chunked," with skill and comprehension tasks integrated throughout.
- Extensive use of graphic organizers aids in note-taking.

EXPLICIT VOCABULARY INSTRUCTION

A targeted approach to vocabulary including
- vocabulary tasks pre- and post-reading and listening
- vocabulary tips and glossing of receptive vocabulary
- a vocabulary strategy section in every chapter
- online reviews with pronunciation practice

GRAMMAR FOR WRITING / SPEAKING

- A dedicated grammar presentation prepares students for authentic writing and speaking tasks.
- Grammar practices in the Student Book and in MyEnglishLab move from controlled to practical application.

SOFT SKILLS

Task-based strategies linked to chapter topics focus on academic success, life skills, and college readiness.

PUTTING STUDENTS ON THE PATH TO *UNIVERSITY SUCCESS*

Intensive skill development and extended application—tied to specific learning outcomes—provide the scaffolding English language learners need to become confident and successful in a university setting.

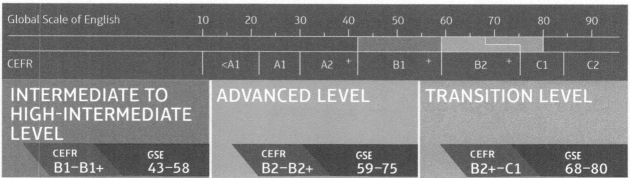

Global Scale of English	10	20	30	40	50	60	70	80	90
CEFR		<A1	A1	A2 +	B1 +	B2 +	C1	C2	

INTERMEDIATE TO HIGH-INTERMEDIATE LEVEL

CEFR B1–B1+ **GSE** 43–58

Authentic content with careful integration of essential skills, the Intermediate to High-Intermediate level familiarizes students with real-world academic contexts.

INTENSIVE SKILL PRACTICE

Intensive skill practice tied to learning objectives informed by the Global Scale of English

AUTHENTIC CONTENT

- Readings: 200–2,000 words
- Lectures: 15–20 minutes
- Multiple exposures and chunking

EXPLICIT VOCABULARY INSTRUCTION

- Pre- and post-reading and listening vocabulary tasks
- Glossing of receptive vocabulary
- Recycling throughout each part and online

SCAFFOLDED APPROACH

Multiple guided exercises focus on comprehension, application, and clarification of productive skills.

VOCABULARY STRATEGIES

Vocabulary strategy sections focus on form, use, and meaning.

GRAPHIC ORGANIZERS

Extensive integration of graphic organizers throughout to support note-taking and help students process complex content.

ADVANCED LEVEL

CEFR B2–B2+ **GSE** 59–75

Challenging, authentic content with level-appropriate skills, the Advanced level prepares students to exit the ESL safety net.

INTENSIVE SKILL PRACTICE

Intensive skill practice tied to learning objectives informed by the Global Scale of English

AUTHENTIC CONTENT

- Readings: 200–3,000 words
- Lectures: 20 minutes

EXPLICIT VOCABULARY INSTRUCTION

- Pre- and post-reading and listening vocabulary tasks
- Glossing of receptive vocabulary
- Recycling throughout each part and online

MODERATELY SCAFFOLDED

Guided exercises focus on comprehension, application, and clarification of productive skills.

VOCABULARY STRATEGIES

Vocabulary strategy sections focus on form, use, and meaning to help students process complex content.

TRANSITION LEVEL

CEFR B2+–C1 **GSE** 68–80

A deep dive for transition-level students, the Transition level mirrors the academic rigor of college courses.

INTENSIVE SKILL PRACTICE

Intensive skill practice tied to learning objectives informed by the Global Scale of English

AUTHENTIC CONTENT

- Readings: 200–3,500-words
- Lectures: 25 minutes

CONTENT AND FLUENCY VOCABULARY APPROACH

- No direct vocabulary instruction
- Online vocabulary practice for remediation

Key Features

A consistent and systematic format in every chapter enables students to build confidence as they master essential fundamental and critical thinking skills.

CHAPTER STRUCTURE

CHAPTER PROFILE
This overview establishes context with visuals to provide interest and schema-building.

OUTCOMES
Sequenced, recycled, and carefully integrated, outcomes focus on developing language skills and are informed by Pearson's Global Scale of English.

GETTING STARTED
A set of discussion questions activates learner schema and motivates students to engage with the content.

READ
The thematically-related readings highlight key concepts. These are accompanied by skill presentation, critical thinking, collaboration, and practical application tasks.

WRITE
Modes for authentic academic writing tasks with careful step-by-step writing instruction, tied to learner outcomes, prepare students to integrate content, grammar, and vocabulary as they move through the stages of the writing process.

GRAMMAR FOR WRITING
Dedicated grammar presentation and practices prepare students for authentic writing tasks.

VOCABULARY STRATEGY
A targeted approach to vocabulary instruction with strategies, previews, and reviews gives students tools to expand their vocabulary.

APPLY YOUR SKILLS
Extensive practical application allows students to practice the skills developed in the chapter.

DEVELOP SOFT SKILLS
Task-based strategies focus on college readiness, social and cultural awareness, and academic study.

Students are engaged from the first page, with unit openers that feature high-interest images related to the chapter themes. Chapter openers include a stimulating, content-based image and an overview of the chapter's topics and skills.

Unit 1 BUSINESS

Money and E-Commerce

| Chapter 1 | Mobile Money | 2 |
| Chapter 2 | A Cashless World | 28 |

Go to **MyEnglishLab** to watch an introduction about BUSINESS.

A **video introduction** at the beginning of each unit by a university professor gives students an academic perspective.

A chapter profile outlines the content with questions to guide students as they learn about the topics.

Outcomes aligned with the Global Scale of English are clearly stated to ensure student awareness of skills.

Chapter 1   Mobile Money

CHAPTER PROFILE

Money and e-commerce is an area of study that looks at how people pay for things and the technology they use. In this chapter, you will study the growing popularity of mobile payments.

You will learn the answers to these questions:

- How has money changed over time?
- What is a mobile payment, and what is good and bad about it?
- Where are mobile payments popular?

For more about MONEY AND E-COMMERCE, see Chapter 2. See also [OC] MONEY AND E-COMMERCE, Chapters 1 and 2.

2   UNIT 1   MONEY AND E-COMMERCE

OUTCOMES

- Preview to predict topics and main ideas
- Express likes and dislikes
- Use connectors in compound sentences
- Guess meaning from context
- Make a budget

Engaging and high-interest readings allow students to connect with the academic content as they develop fundamental reading and critical thinking skills.

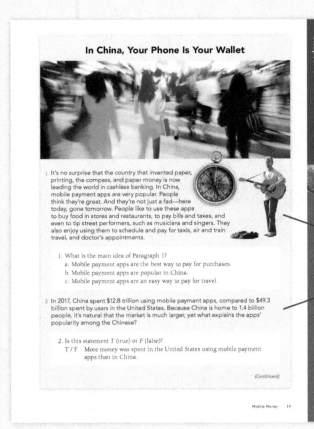

In China, Your Phone Is Your Wallet

1 It's no surprise that the country that invented paper, printing, the compass, and paper money is now leading the world in cashless banking. In China, mobile payment apps are very popular. People think they're great. And they're not just a fad—here today, gone tomorrow. People like to use these apps to buy food in stores and restaurants, to pay bills and taxes, and even to tip street performers, such as musicians and singers. They also enjoy using them to schedule and pay for taxis, air and train travel, and doctor's appointments.

1. What is the main idea of Paragraph 1?
   a. Mobile payment apps are the best way to pay for purchases.
   b. Mobile payment apps are popular in China.
   c. Mobile payment apps are an easy way to pay for travel.

2 In 2017, China spent $12.8 trillion using mobile payment apps, compared to $49.3 billion spent by users in the United States. Because China is home to 1.4 billion people, it's natural that the market is much larger, yet what explains the apps' popularity among the Chinese?

2. Is this statement *T* (true) or *F* (false)?
   T / F More money was spent in the United States using mobile payment apps than in China.

(Continued)

Readings are "chunked" to support the unique needs of beginning students.

Carefully scaffolded language learning **tasks** develop the language skills students need to manage more linguistically complex and conceptually challenging content as they move towards the rigor of college courses.

Tasks follow **Bloom's Taxonomy** to build, develop, and practice skills.

C. Were your predictions in Before You Read correct?

◉ Go to **MyEnglishLab** to reread the article.

D. Reread the article. Answer the questions. Write the number of the paragraph(s) where you found the answers. Discuss your answers with a partner.

1. In China, what goods and services can be paid for with a mobile payment? _____

2. In 2017, how much money was spent in China using mobile payments? _____

3. What reasons explain why mobile payments are popular in China? _____

4. What are two of the most popular mobile payment apps used in China? _____

5. What other countries are now accepting Chinese mobile payment apps? _____

E. Complete the tasks. Discuss your ideas with a partner.

1. How can you preview an article? Circle <u>all</u> correct answers.
   a. Look at the pictures.
   b. Read the first and last sentence of each paragraph.
   c. Read the first and last paragraph.
   d. Look for specific information, such as names and numbers.
   e. Skim the article.
   f. Read each sentence carefully.

2. How can previewing be useful?

VOCABULARY REVIEW

Complete the sentences. Use the words from the box. Use the correct form.

abroad	invent	local	natural	owe	tip

1. Many university students go _____ to travel to a new country and learn about a new culture.

2. At U.S. restaurants, most people _____ the server 15 to 20 percent of the total bill if the service is good.

3. The TV series *Star Trek* introduced many devices before anyone _____ the actual technology.

4. The average university student in the United States _____ $28,400 after graduating. Repaying that money usually takes years.

5. In my grandmother's village, the _____ practice is to pay with cash.

6. It's _____ for customers to prefer apps that are accepted by many businesses. They want convenience.

Writing skills prepare students for the complexity and challenges of the higher levels and authentic academic writing. Writing skills include telling stories using time signals, using descriptive language, using spatial order to describe visuals, and describing a process.

WRITE

SKILL: EXPRESSING LIKES AND DISLIKES

WHY IT'S USEFUL   By expressing likes and dislikes, you can give your opinion about a topic.

In university classes, professors expect you to have opinions about what you read. They may ask you to express this in writing or discussion. One way is to **express what you like or dislike** about the topic. Study the chart.

Express Likes	Express Dislikes
I like …	I don't like …
I enjoy …	I don't like … very much.
I really like …	I dislike …
I think … is very good.	I really don't like …
I love …	I think … is terrible.
	I hate …

Read the student paragraph. Notice the boldfaced expressions.

File   Home   Insert   Page layout   Object   Type

Why I Like Cash

I don't like to spend my money; however, when I do spend money, **I enjoy** using cash. When I use cash, I can see how much money I have to spend. **I really don't like** using a credit card since you can go in debt. For example, I had a friend who used a credit card, and now she is in debt because she spent more than she had. Now **she hates** using credit cards because she owes the credit card company a lot of money. In the future, I might use a mobile payment app because you can connect it to your debit card. As a result, you can only spend what you have in your bank account, and **I like** knowing that the bank is keeping a record of each time I use the card.

REMEMBER

Complete the sentence.

Expressing likes and dislikes is one way to express your _____ about a topic.

Why It's Useful sections highlight the need for developing skills and support transfer of skills to mainstream class content.

Clear and concise **presentations** help students focus on the target skill.

Throughout each chapter, **images** support understanding of vocabulary and concepts.

Writing **models** feature chapter-based writing skill and grammar targets, giving students a reference for upcoming writing tasks.

Students are introduced to the writing process with step-by-step writing instruction, tied to learner outcomes.

WRITE AN OPINION PARAGRAPH
STEP 1: READ TO WRITE
A. Preview the article. What is it about?
B. Read the article. Complete the tasks.

Step 1 exposes students to a **model** of authentic academic writing. The model also serves as additional background information on the topic.

Scan and Go: The Pros and Cons of Mobile Payments

1 The next time you're at Starbucks®, you may be surprised to see someone pay with a smartphone. More and more stores, banks, and governments are offering these mobile payment apps, which connect to a user's bank account. On the other end, who is using these apps, why, and what are the risks?

STEP 2: PREPARE TO WRITE

Prepare to write a short paragraph that expresses your opinion about one of these traditional forms of money: cash, credit card, debit card, or check.

1. A **T-chart** is a graphic organizer that can help you categorize ideas. Study the example.

MY SMARTPHONE

What I Like	What I Dislike
The screen is large.	It's too big for my pocket.
The camera takes good pictures.	There's not enough memory.

Step 2 prepares students for the writing task. Extensive use of **graphic organizers** support students through the writing process.

STEP 3: WRITE

Write your opinion paragraph.

• Look at the ideas in your T-chart and decide what to write about.
• Use expressions of like or dislike.
• Include at least four connectors to combine independent clauses.
• Introduce the main idea in the first sentence. For example:

I really like my smartphone because the screen is large ...

In Step 3, students integrate content, writing skills, grammar, and vocabulary as they move through **the writing process**.

STEP 4: PROOFREAD AND EDIT

A. Read your paragraph and circle any mistakes. Answer the questions in the chart.

Did you ...	Yes	No	Notes
indent your paragraph?			
start each sentence with a capital letter?			
use correct punctuation to end each sentence?			
write about one topic?			
write about likes or dislikes?			
use connectors to combine independent clauses?			

Step 4 guides students through a **self and peer review** process as they expand essential writing skills.

B. Share your paragraph with a partner. Read your partner's paragraph and answer the questions in the chart.

Peer Review Form	Notes
What is the topic of the paragraph? What is the writer's opinion about that topic?	
How many sentences are there?	
Are there at least four connectors used to make compound sentences?	
Is the paragraph formatted correctly? (indented with correct capitalization and punctuation)	
Do you have any questions or comments for the writer?	

Dedicated grammar presentation and practice prepare students for authentic writing tasks. Tasks focus on form, use, and meaning and move from controlled to practical application.

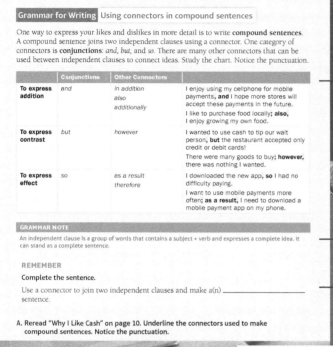

Grammar for Writing Using connectors in compound sentences

One way to express your likes and dislikes in more detail is to write **compound sentences**. A compound sentence joins two independent clauses using a connector. One category of connectors is **conjunctions**: *and*, *but*, and *so*. There are many other connectors that can be used between independent clauses to connect ideas. Study the chart. Notice the punctuation.

	Conjunctions	Other Connectors	
To express addition	*and*	*In addition* *also* *additionally*	I enjoy using my cellphone for mobile payments, **and** I hope more stores will accept these payments in the future. I like to purchase food locally; **also,** I enjoy growing my own food.
To express contrast	*but*	*however*	I wanted to use cash to tip our wait person, **but** the restaurant accepted only credit or debit cards! There were many goods to buy; **however,** there was nothing I wanted.
To express effect	*so*	*as a result* *therefore*	I downloaded the new app, **so** I had no difficulty paying. I want to use mobile payments more often; **as a result,** I need to download a mobile payment app on my phone.

GRAMMAR NOTE

An independent clause is a group of words that contains a subject + verb and expresses a complete idea. It can stand as a complete sentence.

REMEMBER

Complete the sentence.

Use a connector to join two independent clauses and make a(n) _____ sentence.

A. Reread "Why I Like Cash" on page 10. Underline the connectors used to make compound sentences. Notice the punctuation.

Grammar charts feature essential structures with content-based examples and provide support for writing tasks.

Grammar Notes throughout the chapters focus on specific points of syntactic information relevant for beginning students.

Remember boxes allow students to demonstrate understanding of the skill.

Chapter 1

Chapter 2

A. Read the student paragraph. Underline the present perfect.

File   Home   Insert   Page layout   Object   Type   View

Working in a Cashless Restaurant

My sister Layla has worked at a cashless restaurant for two years and loves it. First of all, she is more relaxed. Since starting, she has never worried about someone robbing the store or about making a mistake with the cash accounts. Layla also can spend more time helping customers. As a result, customers are happier. She has made more money from customers' tips since the cashless policy started. For Layla, the cashless restaurant has been the best place to work so far.

Model paragraphs allow students to see the grammar in context and also help build additional background information on the topic.

B. Complete the sentences. Use the present perfect form of the boldfaced verbs.

1. Omar _____ **(eat)** at many different cashless restaurants.

2. In rural areas—where Internet connection may be bad—many people _____ **(not go)** to a cashless restaurant.

3. Jack Ma is a co-founder of Alibaba®—a popular e-commerce site. He _____ **(be)** its executive chairman since 2013.

4. E-commerce websites _____ **(become)** a very popular way to shop for goods and services.

5. Amina _____ **(study)** English for three years but _____ **(never speak)** to a native English speaker.

Multiple grammar exercises encourage application of the grammar target.

C. Find and correct an error with the present perfect or with example language in each sentence.

1. Layla has work at the cashless restaurant for two years.

2. Jeff Bezos started Amazon in 1994 and have been its chairman since then.

3. China has spend a lot of time and money to develop its e-commerce industry.

4. Because of a better Internet connection, many businesses started to accept mobile payments.

5. During his lifetime, Jack Ma has have many different jobs.

6. The woman was successful in many ways. Example, she opened a cashless restaurant.

7. Servers at busy coffee shops, likes Starbucks, are slowed down by customers who pay with cash.

8. The store has many different workers, like as cashiers, servers, and managers.

🔾 Go to **MyEnglishLab** for more grammar practice.

A Cashless World   37

A mix of academic and high-frequency vocabulary provides the fundamental building blocks with which students can read and discern texts and construct meaningful writing.

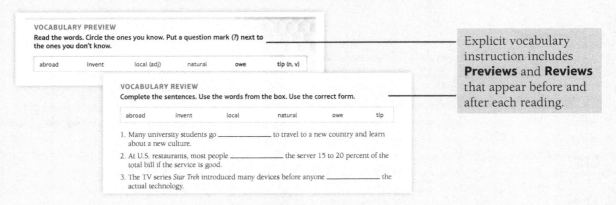

VOCABULARY PREVIEW

Read the words. Circle the ones you know. Put a question mark (?) next to the ones you don't know.

| abroad | invent | local (adj) | natural | owe | tip (n, v) |

VOCABULARY REVIEW

Complete the sentences. Use the words from the box. Use the correct form.

| abroad | invent | local | natural | owe | tip |

1. Many university students go _____ to travel to a new country and learn about a new culture.
2. At U.S. restaurants, most people _____ the server 15 to 20 percent of the total bill if the service is good.
3. The TV series *Star Trek* introduced many devices before anyone _____ the actual technology.

Explicit vocabulary instruction includes **Previews** and **Reviews** that appear before and after each reading.

VOCABULARY STRATEGY

KEEPING A VOCABULARY JOURNAL

WHY IT'S USEFUL By keeping a vocabulary journal, you can better organize and learn new words.

Vocabulary journals are a place to record new words and their meanings. When reading, you will see a lot of new vocabulary. It is important not to stop to look up every unknown word. Instead, underline the word, continue reading, and try to guess its meaning from the context of the sentence or paragraph. Later, you can decide which words you want to learn and record them in your vocabulary journal. A simple vocabulary journal entry will contain the word and its definition.

In addition to showing the word and definition, a vocabulary journal entry can also include the following:

- part of speech (noun, verb, adjective, adverb, etc.)
- word family members: words with the same root but different beginnings (prefixes) and endings (suffixes)
- the word in context: the sentence that the word originally was in (from the reading)
- your own example sentence with the word

Consider a student's vocabulary journal entry for the word *retailer*.

Word: retailer
Definition: a person or company that sells things to people in shops
Part of speech: noun
Word family: retail (n), retail (adj)
Word in context: Because it saves them money, unstaffed shopping is popular with **retailers**.
Your own sentence: Amazon is one of the biggest e-commerce **retailers**.

Knowing the word, noticing how it's used, and using it in your own words will help grow your vocabulary knowledge. Be sure to review your vocabulary journal so that you remember your new words.

Vocabulary Strategies offer valuable tools for recognizing, expanding, and retaining vocabulary.

Strategies include: guessing meaning from context, keeping a vocabulary journal, identifying collocations, and using graphic organizers to learn vocabulary.

Tips throughout the chapter include helpful information and additional scaffolding to support beginning students.

TIP

To *predict* is to make a guess about what will happen next. To understand new information more quickly, make predictions before and while you read. Before you read, ask yourself: "From what I know about the topic, what could the reading be about? While you read, ask: What will happen next?"

Each chapter concludes with an Apply Your Skills section that includes practical applications. This section can also function as an assessment.

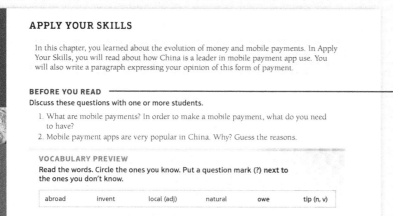

APPLY YOUR SKILLS

In this chapter, you learned about the evolution of money and mobile payments. In Apply Your Skills, you will read about how China is a leader in mobile payment app use. You will also write a paragraph expressing your opinion of this form of payment.

BEFORE YOU READ

Discuss these questions with one or more students.

1. What are mobile payments? In order to make a mobile payment, what do you need to have?
2. Mobile payment apps are very popular in China. Why? Guess the reasons.

VOCABULARY PREVIEW

Read the words. Circle the ones you know. Put a question mark (?) next to the ones you don't know.

abroad	invent	local (adj)	natural	owe	tip (n, v)

🔊 Go to **MyEnglishLab** to complete a vocabulary practice.

READ

A. Preview the article "Your Phone Is Your Wallet" on the next page. What is it about?

B. Read the article. Answer the questions

Glossary

availability: being able to be used or seen
convenience: the quality of being useful, helpful, or easy
expand: to become larger or make something larger
traditionally: being done in a particular way for a long time
worry (n): the feeling of being unhappy or anxious about something

A **Before You Read** activity gives students the opportunity to discuss questions related to the topic of their final assignment.

This **longer reading passage** allows students to apply skills practiced in the chapter.

Cashless Societies—Good for All?

1 In 2016, Prime Minister Narendra Modi of India ordered the removal of the 1,000 rupee note (valued at about $14.50). Most Indians were upset and ran to the bank to exchange their money before it became useless. Modi's idea was to fight corruption and tax evasion, but the result was something else: Millions of Indians joined the digital economy.

1. Prime Minister Narendra Modi ordered the removal of the _____ rupee note.
   a. 200   b. 1,000   c. 2,000

Think Critically asks students to engage at a deep level with the content.

THINK CRITICALLY

In the article "In China, Your Phone Is Your Wallet," you read some reasons why mobile payment apps are popular in China. Use information from the article to answer the questions. Then discuss your ideas with a partner.

1. Are mobile payment apps popular in your home country? What are the reasons? Explain.
   _____
   _____

Think Visually provides an opportunity for students to analyze visuals, graphs, and charts.

THINK VISUALLY

The bar chart shows the number of people who use popular mobile payment apps. Use information from the chart to answer the questions. Then discuss your ideas with a partner.

1. Which mobile payment app is the most popular? What do you know about this company?
   _____
   _____

Strategies for academic success, life skills, and career readiness skills—including asking for research help at a library, communicating appropriately online, making healthy food choices, and giving presentations—appear in each chapter. These soft skills help increase students' confidence and ability to cope with the challenges of academic study and college culture. Soft skills are linked to topics in the chapters.

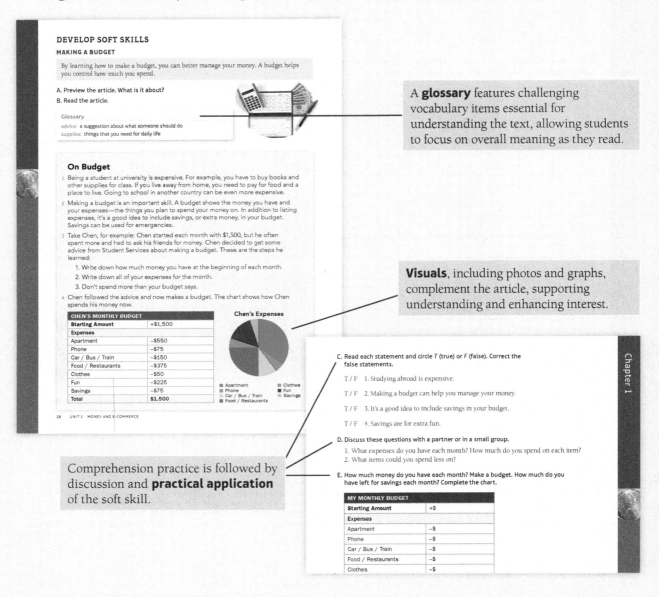

DEVELOP SOFT SKILLS

MAKING A BUDGET

By learning how to make a budget, you can better manage your money. A budget helps you control how much you spend.

A. Preview the article. What is it about?

B. Read the article.

Glossary

advice: a suggestion about what someone should do
supplies: things that you need for daily life

A **glossary** features challenging vocabulary items essential for understanding the text, allowing students to focus on overall meaning as they read.

On Budget

1 Being a student at university is expensive. For example, you have to buy books and other supplies for class. If you live away from home, you need to pay for food and a place to live. Going to school in another country can be even more expensive.

2 Making a budget is an important skill. A budget shows the money you have and your expenses—the things you plan to spend your money on. In addition to listing expenses, it's a good idea to include savings, or extra money, in your budget. Savings can be used for emergencies.

3 Take Chen, for example: Chen started each month with $1,500, but he often spent more and had to ask his friends for money. Chen decided to get some advice from Student Services about making a budget. These are the steps he learned:

   1. Write down how much money you have at the beginning of each month.
   2. Write down all of your expenses for the month.
   3. Don't spend more than your budget says.

4 Chen followed the advice and now makes a budget. The chart shows how Chen spends his money now.

CHEN'S MONTHLY BUDGET	
Starting Amount	+$1,500
Expenses	
Apartment	−$550
Phone	−$75
Car / Bus / Train	−$150
Food / Restaurants	−$375
Clothes	−$50
Fun	−$225
Savings	−$75
Total	**$1,500**

Chen's Expenses

■ Apartment   ■ Clothes
■ Phone   ■ Fun
■ Car / Bus / Train   ■ Savings
■ Food / Restaurants

26   UNIT 1 MONEY AND E-COMMERCE

Visuals, including photos and graphs, complement the article, supporting understanding and enhancing interest.

C. Read each statement and circle *T* (true) or *F* (false). Correct the false statements.

T / F   1. Studying abroad is expensive.

T / F   2. Making a budget can help you manage your money.

T / F   3. It's a good idea to include savings in your budget.

T / F   4. Savings are for extra fun.

D. Discuss these questions with a partner or in a small group.

   1. What expenses do you have each month? How much do you spend on each item?
   2. What items could you spend less on?

E. How much money do you have each month? Make a budget. How much do you have left for savings each month? Complete the chart.

MY MONTHLY BUDGET	
Starting Amount	+$
Expenses	
Apartment	−$
Phone	−$
Car / Bus / Train	−$
Food / Restaurants	−$
Clothes	−$

Chapter 1

Comprehension practice is followed by discussion and **practical application** of the soft skill.

At the end of each chapter, students complete a **skill self-assessment** checklist.

WHAT DID YOU LEARN?

Read the sentences. Check (✓) what you learned.

☐ I can preview to predict topics and main ideas.

☐ I can express likes and dislikes.

☐ I can use connectors in compound sentences.

☐ I can guess meaning from context.

☐ I can make a budget.

◐ Go to **MyEnglishLab** to complete a self-assessment.

Mobile Money   27

A BLENDED APPROACH

University Success integrates a tailored online lab populated with engaging multimedia content including videos, slide presentations, and audio, which can be used for presenting new content and skills, as well as practice and extension activities for students to complete in class or as homework. All MyEnglishLab activities are referenced throughout the Student Books.

MyEnglishLab includes an easy-to-use online management system that offers a flexible gradebook and tools for monitoring student success.

TEACHER RESOURCES

Downloadable step-by-step teaching notes for each chapter offer suggestions and a "library" of teaching tips for teaching skills and content

Essential tools such as audio scripts, answer keys, and course planners help in lesson planning

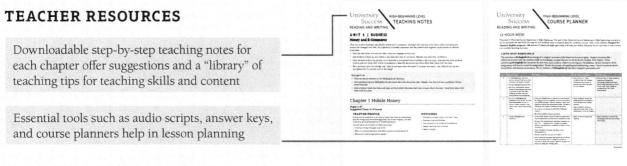

ASSESSMENT PROGRAM

University Success has several different types of assessments that provide opportunities for teachers to gauge learning. These assessments can be used as pre-course diagnostics, chapter achievement tests, mid-course assessments, and final summative assessments. The flexible nature of these assessments allows teachers to choose which assessments will be most appropriate at various stages of the program. Two different versions of these assessments are available in MyEnglishLab, in both Word and PDF formats. There are formative assessments embedded in the Student Book.

HOW WOULD YOU LIKE TO ASSESS YOUR STUDENTS?

Assessment	Where to Find	How to Use
Skill Self-Assessments	MyEnglishLab	• At the beginning and end of every chapter for students to identify skill areas for improvement • To provide data that can inform lesson planning
Achievement Tests	MyEnglishLab	• As a summative assessment at the end of each chapter
Apply Your Skills	Student Book	• As a diagnostic assessment to inform students' strengths and weaknesses before they complete a chapter • As a formative assessment, in which students complete this section or parts of this section after they complete the chapter
Mid-Term Exam	MyEnglishLab	• As a summative assessment at the end of Units 1 and 2
Final Exam	MyEnglsihLab	• As a summative assessment at the end of Units 3 and 4
Writing / Speaking Skill Assessment	Student Book	• Writing and Speaking Tasks: As formative assessments to evaluate practical application of skills presented
Vocabulary Quiz	Student Book	• *Vocabulary Previews / Reviews:* As a diagnostic to inform teaching and lesson planning • As formative assessments to assess student understanding of vocabulary
Grammar Quiz	Student Book	• *Grammar tasks:* As a diagnostic to identify student understanding of grammar points • As formative assessments to assess student understanding of grammar points
Skill, Vocabulary, Grammar Assessments	MyEnglishLab	• Any activity in MyEnglishLab to be used as formative assessments to assess student understanding of chapter-related content

Scope and Sequence

	READING SKILLS	WRITING SKILLS

GRAMMAR SKILLS	VOCABULARY STRATEGIES	SOFT SKILLS	MYENGLISHLAB
			Video: An Introduction about Business
Use connectors in compound sentences	Guess meaning from context	Make a budget TASK Look at your monthly expenses and make a budget	Skill self-assessments Online practice: • reading • grammar • vocabulary
Use the present perfect	Keep a vocabulary journal	Protect your money TASK Create a list of ways to protect your money online	Skill self-assessments Online practice: • reading • grammar • vocabulary Challenge reading: **Unstaffed Businesses of Yesterday and Today**
			Video: An Introduction about Humanities
Use modals to express ability, possibility, and permission	Use a dictionary to learn new words	Understand professor feedback TASK Role-play a conversation between a student and professor about feedback	Skill self-assessments Online practice: • reading • grammar • vocabulary
Describe cause-and-effect relationships	Identify collocations	Communicate with your professors TASK Draft an email to a professor about an issue you want to discuss	Skill self-assessments Online practice: • reading • grammar • vocabulary Challenge reading: **Sharing Your Stories**
			Video: An Introduction about Structural Science
Use adverbs of frequency	Build word families with suffixes	Give presentations TASK Create a slide presentation based on a paragraph that you wrote	Skill self-assessments Online practice: • reading • grammar • vocabulary
Use the comparative form of adjectives	Build word families with prefixes	Work in groups TASK Identify problems and solutions for working in groups	Skill self-assessments Online practice: • reading • grammar • vocabulary Challenge reading: **Learning with Legos**
			Video: An Introduction about Natural Science
Use the superlative form of adjectives	Use word maps	Volunteer your time TASK Research volunteer opportunities at your school or in your area	Skill self-assessments Online practice: • reading • grammar • vocabulary
Use count and noncount nouns	Create alphaboxes	Solve problems TASK Brainstorm solutions to problems that you need help with	Skill self-assessments Online practice: • reading • grammar • vocabulary Challenge reading: **Big Business and Sustainable Agriculture: An Unlikely Pair**

Acknowledgments

Many thanks to the incredible team at Pearson: Amy McCormick, Niki Lee, Sarah Hand, and untold others who supported and worked tirelessly on this project. Special thanks to Debbie Sistino, who carefully guided this project from start to finish. Heartful thanks goes to Leigh Stolle, my editor, who I was extremely fortunate to team up with again. Leigh's insight, expertise, and spot-on feedback shaped this book into what it is today.

I am lucky to teach at Union County College, whose ESL students and teachers always inspire me in my teaching and material writing. Writing a textbook while raising a young family is a juggling act, so I'm eternally thankful to my parents for all their help with looking after the kids. Finally, to Carlos, Sophia, and Lucas: Thank you for your love, patience, and support while I spent all those hours writing from home. I appreciate all the sacrifices you make. Sophia: Your feedback on leveling these readings was invaluable, and I'm so proud that you played a role in the creation of this book.

—Carrie Steenburgh

Reviewers

We would like to thank the following reviewers for their many helpful comments and suggestions:

Jamila Barton, North Seattle Community College, Seattle, WA; **Joan Chamberlin**, Iowa State University, Ames IA; **Lyam Christopher**, Palm Beach State College, Boynton Beach, FL; **Robin Corcos**, University of California, Santa Barbara, Goleta, CA; **Tanya Davis**, University of California, San Diego, CA; **Brendan DeCoster**, University of Oregon, Eugene, OR; **Thomas Dougherty**, University of St. Mary of the Lake, Mundelein, IL; **Bina Dugan**, Bergen County Community College, Hackensack, NJ; **Bonnie Duhart**, Lone Star College, University Park, TX; **Priscilla Faucette**, University of Hawaii at Manoa, Honolulu, HI; **Lisa Fischer**, St. Louis University, St. Louis, MO; **Kathleen Flynn**, Glendale Community College, Glendale, CA; **Mary Gawienowski**, William Rainey Harper College, Palatine, IL; **Sally Gearhart**, Santa Rosa Junior College, Santa Rosa, CA; **Carl Guerriere**, Capital Community College, Hartford, CT; **Vera Guillen**, Eastfield College, Mesquite, TX; **Angela Hakim**, St. Louis University, St. Louis, MO; **Pamela Hartmann**, Evans Community Adult School, Los Angeles Unified School District, Los Angeles, CA; **Shelly Hedstrom**, Palm Beach State University, Lake Worth, FL; **Sherie Henderson**, University of Oregon, Eugene, OR; **Lisse Hildebrandt**, English Language Program, Virginia Commonwealth University, Richmond, VA; **Barbara Inerfeld**, Rutgers University, Piscataway, NJ; **Bessie Karras-Lazaris**, California State University, Northridge, CA; **Zaimah Khan**, Northern Virginia Community College, Loudon Campus, Sterling, VA; **Tricia Kinman**, St. Louis University, St. Louis, MO; **Kathleen Klaiber**, Genesee Community College, Batavia, NY; **Kevin Lamkins**, Capital Community College, Hartford, CT; **Noga Laor**, Long Island University, Brooklyn, NY; **Mayetta Lee**, Palm Beach State College, Lake Worth, FL; **Kirsten Lillegard**, English Language Institute, Divine Word College, Epworth, IA; **Craig Machado**, Norwalk Community College, Norwalk, CT; **Cheryl Madrid**, Spring International Language Center, Denver, CO; **Ann Meechai**, St. Louis University, St. Louis, MO; **Melissa Mendelson**, Department of Linguistics, University of Utah, Salt Lake City, UT; **Tamara Milbourn**, University of Colorado, Boulder, CO; **Debbie Ockey**, Fresno City College, Fresno, CA; **Diana Pascoe-Chavez**, St. Louis University, St. Louis, MO; **Raymond Purdy**, ELS Language Centers, Princeton, NJ; **Kathleen Reynolds**, William Rainey Harper College, Palatine, IL; **Linda Roth**, Vanderbilt University ELC, Greensboro, NC; **Minati Roychoudhuri**, Capital Community College, Hartford, CT; **Bruce Rubin**, California State University, Fullerton, CA; **Margo Sampson**, Syracuse University, Syracuse, NY; **Elena Sapp**, Oregon State University, Corvallis, OR; **Sarah Saxer**, Howard Community College, Ellicott City, MD; **Anne-Marie Schlender**, Austin Community College, Austin, TX; **Susan Shields**, Santa Barbara Community College, Santa Barbara, CA; **Barbara Smith-Palinkas**, Hillsborough Community College, Dale Mabry Campus, Tampa, FL; **Sara Stapleton**, North Seattle Community College, Seattle, WA; **Lisa Stelle**, Northern Virginia Community College Loudon, Sterling, VA; **Jamie Tanzman**, Northern Kentucky University, Highland Heights, KY; **Ariana Van Beurden**, Oregon State University, Corvallis, OR; **Jeffrey Welliver**, Soka University of America, Aliso Viejo, CA; **Mark Wolfersberger**, Brigham Young University, Hawaii, Laie, HI; **May Youn**, California State University, Fullerton, CA

Money and E-Commerce

➤ Go to **MyEnglishLab** to watch an introduction about **BUSINESS**.

1

Chapter 1   Mobile Money

CHAPTER PROFILE

Money and e-commerce is an area of study that looks at how people pay for things and the technology they use. In this chapter, you will study the growing popularity of mobile payments.

You will learn the answers to these questions:

- How has money changed over time?

- What is a mobile payment, and what is good and bad about it?

- Where are mobile payments popular?

For more about **MONEY AND E-COMMERCE**, see Chapter 2. See also [OC] **MONEY AND E-COMMERCE**, Chapters 1 and 2.

OUTCOMES

- Preview to predict topics and main ideas

- Express likes and dislikes

- Use connectors in compound sentences

- Guess meaning from context

- Make a budget

GETTING STARTED

Discuss these questions with a partner or in a small group.

1. Look at the picture on page 2. How is the person paying? What are other ways to pay?

2. How do you usually pay for things? Rank them. Write 1 for usually, 2 for sometimes, 3 for not often.

   _____ cash (coins / bills)

   _____ card (debit / credit)

   _____ mobile payment (a mobile phone app like Alipay™, Apple Pay®, PayPal®)

3. Look at the pictures below. How did people pay for things in the past? Check (✓) your ideas.

☐ gold　　　　☐ salt　　　　☐ shells　　　　☐ furs　　　　☐ spices

◑ Go to **MyEnglishLab** to complete a self-assessment.

READ

SKILL: PREVIEWING TO PREDICT TOPICS AND MAIN IDEAS

WHY IT'S USEFUL By previewing, you can predict the topic and main idea of a reading before you start to read.

You will better understand a reading if you can **predict** (guess) the topic and main idea before you read. The **topic** is what the reading is generally about—for example, mobile phone apps. The **main idea** expresses a particular idea about the topic—for example, why the apps are popular. Make predictions by **previewing the reading**.

How to Preview

- Look at **pictures** (photos, maps, diagrams, illustrations) and captions (information under pictures).
- Read the **title** and **headings**.
- Read the **first** and **last sentence** of each paragraph.
- Read the **first** and **last paragraph**. Many writers will express the main idea in the first paragraph and then repeat it in the last paragraph.
- Quickly **skim** (run your eyes quickly over) the whole reading (all of it). Don't read every word and don't stop to look up words. Mark them to look up later.

Try previewing.

- First, look at the pictures in the article "Money Around the World: Same Look, Different Value."
- Next, read the title and the first sentence.
- Then try to answer the questions below the article.
- Read how another student answered. Do you agree?

Money Around the World: Same Look, Different Value

1 Dinar, dollar, peso—almost every country has its own money. Some countries call their money by the same name, but the money is not the same in looks or value.

2 For example, Kuwait, Libya, Jordan, and Iraq each calls its money the *dinar*. But in each country, the dinar looks different and can't always buy the same things. For instance, in Kuwait, the 20-dinar bill shows a palace and a boat and will get you seven tickets at a movie theater. But in Jordan, the 20-dinar bill shows a past king and is enough for three tickets at a movie theater there.

3 The same is true for the dollar bill. In the United States, the 20-dollar bill has a past president on the front and is good for about two movie tickets. However, the Australian 20-dollar bill shows a successful businesswoman and will get you only one movie ticket in Australia.

So even though two bills may share the same name, don't expect to spend an Australian dollar in America or a Kuwaiti dinar in Jordan—it won't be accepted.

Top left: A Kuwaiti 20-dinar bill; Top right: A Jordanian 20-dinar bill with Hussein bin Talal, king of Jordan (1952–1999); Bottom left: A US 20-dollar bill with Andrew Jackson, US president (1829–1837); Bottom right: An Australian 20-dollar bill with Mary Reibey (1777–1855), owner of many farms and a shipping business

1. What is the topic? *money*

2. What is the main idea?
   - ☐ the history of different money around the world
   - ☑ how the look of money differs by country
   - ☐ why the dinar is popular in the Middle East

REMEMBER

Circle the correct answer.

Preview to _____ a reading.

a. guess the topic and main idea of
b. find details (specific information) in
c. learn new vocabulary from

CULTURE NOTE

In US dollars (as of 2019):
1 Kuwaiti dinar = $3.30
1 Jordanian dinar = $1.40
1 Australian dollar = $.70

VOCABULARY PREVIEW

Read the words. Circle the ones you know. Put a question mark (?) next to the ones you don't know.

arrive	goods and services	often	purchase (v)
close (adv)	material	payment	valuable (adj)

● Go to **MyEnglishLab** to complete a vocabulary practice.

PREDICT

Preview the article "The Evolution of Money" on the next page. Complete the tasks.

1. Look at the pictures and title. What is the topic of the article? Circle your prediction.

    banking   spices   money

2. Reread the title and read the first and last sentence of each paragraph. What is the main idea? Check (✓) your prediction.
    - ☐ the ways that people are paid for their work
    - ☐ why mobile payments are better than cash
    - ☐ how the form of money has changed over time

> **TIP**
>
> To *predict* is to make a guess about what will happen next. To understand new information more quickly, make predictions before and while you read. Before you read, ask yourself: "From what I know about the topic, what could the reading be about? While you read, ask: What will happen next?"

A. Read the article. Do not stop to look up words. Answer the questions.

Glossary

emperor: a ruler of a big country or several countries

evolution: the gradual development of an idea, situation, or object

silk: a soft shiny cloth made from thin threads

technology: all the knowledge and equipment used in science, the making of machines, etc.

The Evolution of Money

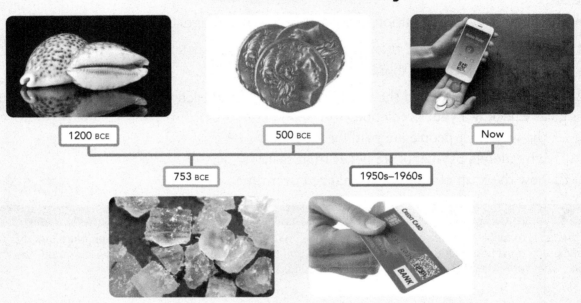

1200 BCE 500 BCE Now

753 BCE 1950s–1960s

1 Shells, salt, coins, credit cards—these have all been used as forms of money. As times change, so does how people pay for things. Therefore, it's not surprising that a new form of money has arrived.

2 Hundreds of years ago, cowry shells were a popular form of payment in areas close to the Indian and Pacific Oceans. These shells, used to decorate clothing and jewelry, were traded throughout the world. In countries where cowry shells were not common—China, for example—they were even more valuable. In fact, early Chinese emperors were often buried with a cowry shell placed inside their mouth.

1. What is the main idea of Paragraph 1?
   a. Shells and salt were a popular form of money.
   b. The form of money changes over time.
   c. People like to pay with credit cards.

2. Read the first sentence of Paragraph 3. Predict the topic.
   a. spices and gold
   b. the Roman Empire
   c. salt as payment

3 Salt, now mostly used to make food taste better, was very valuable in the past. In Roman times, for example, soldiers were paid in salt. People used it to make food taste better and to make it last longer. They also used it for health reasons and traded it for silk, spices, and even gold.

3. Read the first sentence of Paragraph 4. What topic will be explained?
   a. coins
   b. Turkey
   c. China

4 Next came coins, made starting in the 6th century BCE in what is today Turkey. The material used depended on where the coin was made. In Turkey, for instance, early coins were made of silver or gold. In China, bronze was often used.

4. What is the main idea of Paragraph 4?
   a. Turkey was the first country to make coins.
   b. China used bronze to make coins.
   c. Coins became a popular form of payment in the 6th century BCE.

(Continued)

CULTURE NOTE

The Roman Empire started in 27 BCE and ended in 476 CE. During its most powerful period (around 117 CE), the Roman Empire included much of modern-day Western Europe and some countries of the Middle East. In addition to salt, Roman soldiers also received coins. They used the coins to pay for food and other expenses. They also sent the coins back home, to their families.

5 Introduced in the 1950s and 60s, the credit card and debit card changed how people paid for things. Instead of having to carry heavy coins and dirty bills, many people started to use a card to purchase items.

6 Thanks to technology, now *that* is changing. On the timeline of money's evolution, we are at the start of the digital money period—that is, the use of mobile phone apps like Alipay and PayPal to "pay" for goods and services. Some people predict that this is another step toward living in a cashless world.

5. What is the topic of Paragraph 5?

   a. credit and debit cards

   b. the 1950s and 60s

   c. coins and bills

6. What is the main idea of the article?

   a. Forms of payment have changed over time.

   b. Shells and salt were popular payments of the past.

   c. Credit and debit cards are most popular now.

B. Were your predictions in Predict correct? What helped you predict the main idea?

◑ Go to **MyEnglishLab** to reread the article.

C. Reread the article. Then read each statement and circle *T* (true) or *F* (false). Correct the false statements.

T / F   1. Fish, salt, coins, and cards are forms of payment discussed in the article.

T / F   2. People wore cowry shells as decoration and used them like money.

T / F   3. Cowry shells were used in places around the Atlantic and Pacific Oceans.

T / F   4. During the Roman Empire, soldiers were paid in salt.

T / F   5. The first coin was made in the area that is now the country of Turkey.

T / F   6. Coins were always made from the same material.

T / F   7. One reason people use credit cards is because they don't like to carry cash.

T / F   8. Digital technology is the use of apps to pay for things.

Grammar for Writing   Using connectors in compound sentences

One way to express your likes and dislikes in more detail is to write **compound sentences**. A compound sentence joins two independent clauses using a connector. One category of connectors is **conjunctions**: *and, but,* and *so.* There are many other connectors that can be used between independent clauses to connect ideas. Study the chart. Notice the punctuation.

	Conjunctions	Other Connectors	
To express addition	*and*	*in addition* *also* *additionally*	I enjoy using my cellphone for mobile payments**, and** I hope more stores will accept these payments in the future. I like to purchase food locally**; also,** I enjoy growing my own food.
To express contrast	*but*	*however*	I wanted to use cash to tip our wait person**, but** the restaurant accepted only credit or debit cards! There were many goods to buy**; however,** there was nothing I wanted.
To express effect	*so*	*as a result* *therefore*	I downloaded the new app, **so** I had no difficulty paying. I want to use mobile payments more often**; as a result,** I need to download a mobile payment app on my phone.

GRAMMAR NOTE

An independent clause is a group of words that contains a subject + verb and expresses a complete idea. It can stand as a complete sentence.

REMEMBER

Complete the sentence.

Use a connector to join two independent clauses and make a(n) _____ sentence.

A. Reread "Why I Like Cash" on page 10. Underline the connectors used to make compound sentences. Notice the punctuation.

The connectors *in addition, also, additionally, however, as a result,* and *therefore* can also be used to start a sentence. Be sure to use a comma (,) after them.

B. Combine the independent clauses to make compound sentences. Use connectors from the chart on page 11. Try to use a different connector for each sentence. Use the correct punctuation. More than one correct answer may be possible.

1. More and more people enjoy using mobile payment apps / More shops now accept them

   More and more people enjoy using mobile apps; therefore, more shops now accept them.

   or *More and more people enjoy using mobile apps. Therefore, more shops now accept them.*

2. I think having a credit card can be convenient / It's important to use it wisely

   _____

   _____

3. I like to purchase airline tickets with my credit card / I earn reward points for travel

   _____

   _____

4. My sister likes valuable jewelry / She never buys any pieces from infomercials

   _____

   _____

5. Martin's Marketplace has a variety of goods / It doesn't sell medicine

   _____

   _____

6. I dislike the material of my clerk uniform / The color is ugly

   _____

   _____

C. Complete the sentences with your own ideas. Use the connectors from the box.

and	however	in addition	so	therefore

1. I like to use credit cards _____

   _____ .

2. I enjoy shopping online _____

   _____ .

3. My friend really doesn't like to do homework _____

   _____ .

⬥ Go to **MyEnglishLab** for more grammar practice.

WRITE AN OPINION PARAGRAPH

STEP 1: READ TO WRITE

A. Preview the article. What is it about?

B. Read the article. Complete the tasks.

> **Glossary**
>
> **battery:** an object that provides electricity for a radio, car, etc.
>
> **benefit (n):** something that helps you or gives you an advantage
>
> **communication:** the exchange of information
>
> **earn:** to get something because of your actions
>
> **grow up:** to change from being a child to being a man or woman
>
> **hack (v):** to secretly get information from someone's computer
>
> **offer (v):** to show that you are willing to give something to someone
>
> **user:** someone who uses a product, service, etc.

Scan and Go: The Pros and Cons of Mobile Payments

1 The next time you're at Starbucks®, you may be surprised to see someone pay with a smartphone. More and more stores, banks, and governments are offering these mobile payment apps, which connect to a user's bank account. On the other end, who is using these apps, why, and what are the risks?

1. What three questions does the author ask? Underline them and circle the connector.

2 ¹Age tells the story of who likes *m-wallets*, as mobile phone apps are called. ²Many millennials and Generation Zers own smartphones. ³They have grown up with mobile technology; therefore, they are comfortable with it. ⁴In addition, they enjoy the benefits these apps offer. ⁵For instance, users of the Starbucks app can earn free food and drinks. ⁶Finally, this generation is used to fast communication, so it loves the speed of m-wallets. ⁷Just scan your phone and go.

2. Which two compound sentences are connected with a connector? Circle TWO answers.

   a. Sentence 2   c. Sentence 5

   b. Sentence 3   d. Sentence 6

(Continued)

3 ¹These benefits seem great; however, some people don't agree. ²They like their privacy and really dislike the idea of losing it. ³They worry that the store might share their data, or the m-wallet provider could be hacked. ⁴Others worry about theft. ⁵People often misplace their phones, so the money could be stolen. ⁶And some hate the idea of a dead battery. ⁷Money may be in the account, but a dead battery means they can't get to it. ⁸Mobile payment providers will have to work hard to get these people to change from cash to app.

3. Which two sentences have connectors that have the same meaning? Circle TWO answers.

a. Sentence 1

c. Sentence 5

b. Sentence 3

d. Sentence 7

CULTURE NOTE

Millennials are people born between the years 1980 and 1994. Generation Zers are people born between 1995 and 2012.

⊙ Go to **MyEnglishLab** to reread the article.

STEP 2: PREPARE TO WRITE

Prepare to write a short paragraph that expresses your opinion about one of these traditional forms of money: cash, credit card, debit card, or check.

1. A **T-chart** is a graphic organizer that can help you categorize ideas. Study the example.

MY SMARTPHONE	
What I Like	What I Dislike
The screen is large.	It's too big for my pocket.
The camera takes good pictures.	There's not enough memory.

2. Choose your topic—the form of money. Then list what you like and dislike about that topic in the T-chart.

FORM OF MONEY: _____	
What I Like	What I Dislike

STEP 3: WRITE

Write your opinion paragraph.

- Look at the ideas in your T-chart and decide what to write about.
- Use expressions of like or dislike.
- Include at least four connectors to combine independent clauses.
- Introduce the main idea in the first sentence. For example:

I really like my smartphone because the screen is large ...

TIP

Remember, paragraphs are often indented, which means that they start farther in on the page than the rest of the article. Also, all sentences should start with a capital letter and end with correct punctuation. In academic writing, end punctuation is usually a period.

STEP 4: PROOFREAD AND EDIT

A. Read your paragraph and circle any mistakes. Answer the questions in the chart.

Did you ...	Yes	No	Notes
indent your paragraph?			
start each sentence with a capital letter?			
use correct punctuation to end each sentence?			
write about one topic?			
write about likes or dislikes?			
use connectors to combine independent clauses?			

B. Share your paragraph with a partner. Read your partner's paragraph and answer the questions in the chart.

Peer Review Form	Notes
What is the topic of the paragraph? What is the writer's opinion about that topic?	
How many sentences are there?	
Are there at least four connectors used to make compound sentences?	
Is the paragraph formatted correctly? (indented with correct capitalization and punctuation)	
Do you have any questions or comments for the writer?	

C. Share the feedback with your partner. Ask questions about your partner's paragraph. For example:

Why do you like or dislike _____ ?

What form of payment do you use to pay for small items, like food and bus fare?

What form of payment do you use to pay for big items, like school tuition and trips?

Do your parents or older relatives like to use the same form of payment as you?

D. Discuss these questions with a partner or in a small group.

Is it easy to write about your likes and dislikes? Why is writing about likes and dislikes useful?

VOCABULARY STRATEGY

GUESSING MEANING FROM CONTEXT

WHY IT'S USEFUL By guessing meaning from context, you can read faster, making reading more enjoyable.

In your university classes, you will read a lot. Those readings will have unknown vocabulary words, but good readers do not stop to look up every new word. Instead, they try to **guess the meaning of the word from the context**. Here is how:

- Notice how the word is used in the sentence.
- Look at the nearby words.
- Think about what you already know about the topic.

In a reading, the author might provide some *context clues*. These are bits of information that can help you guess the meaning of a word. Study the chart.

Type of Context Clue	
Definition or synonym (a word with a similar meaning) – usually comes after a comma, dash, or colon, or is in parentheses	In China, mobile payment apps are very popular, and they're not just a **fad**—here today, gone tomorrow.
Example – usually comes after *for example, for instance, such as*, etc.	People use mobile payment apps to buy food in stores and restaurants, to pay bills and taxes, and even to tip **street performers**, such as musicians or singers.
Contrast or antonym (a word with an opposite meaning) – usually comes after a comma, dash, or colon, or is in parentheses	For Chinese traveling **abroad**, not just in their own country, it's an easy way to spend money.

A. Use context clues to understand the boldfaced word. What type of context clue is it? Circle the answer. What part of the sentence helped you? Underline it.

1. It's no surprise that the country that **invented**—that is, first imagined and made—paper money is now leading the world in cashless banking.
   a. definition / synonym   b. example   c. antonym / contrast

2. Instead of changing their **yuan** (Chinese money) to the local money, they can use their mobile wallet.
   a. definition / synonym   b. example   c. antonym / contrast

3. Alipay and WeChat Pay™ have **expanded** into countries that are popular with tourists. For instance, Malaysia, France, and South Africa now accept Alipay.
   a. definition / synonym   b. example   c. antonym / contrast

4. Unlike the tourists, the **local** people use cash.
   a. definition / synonym   b. example   c. antonym / contrast

B. Read each sentence. Then guess and write the meaning of each boldfaced word based on context.

1. Many **millennials** (born 1980–1994) and Generation Zers own smartphones.
   Meaning: _____

2. They fear the loss of **privacy**. For example, the store might sell their data.
   Meaning: _____

3. A dead **battery**, which powers the phone, means app users can't get to their money.
   Meaning: _____

4. Mobile payment providers will have to work hard to get these people to **switch**—in other words, change a lifelong habit—from cash to app.
   Meaning: _____

C. Think about the questions. Then share answers with a partner.

1. Do you have similar meanings for the words in Part B? What context clues helped you to guess the meaning of the word?
2. How often do you look up a word in a dictionary or thesaurus when reading in your first language? How often do you look up a word when reading in English? How can using a dictionary be useful? How can using a dictionary be unhelpful?

APPLY YOUR SKILLS

In this chapter, you learned about the evolution of money and mobile payments. In Apply Your Skills, you will read about how China is a leader in mobile payment app use. You will also write a paragraph expressing your opinion of this form of payment.

BEFORE YOU READ

Discuss these questions with one or more students.

1. What are mobile payments? In order to make a mobile payment, what do you need to have?
2. Mobile payment apps are very popular in China. Why? Guess the reasons.

VOCABULARY PREVIEW

Read the words. Circle the ones you know. Put a question mark (?) next to the ones you don't know.

abroad	invent	local (adj)	natural	owe	tip (n, v)

◐ Go to **MyEnglishLab** to complete a vocabulary practice.

READ

A. Preview the article "Your Phone Is Your Wallet" on the next page. What is it about?

B. Read the article. Answer the questions.

Glossary

availability: being able to be used or seen
convenience: the quality of being useful, helpful, or easy
expand: to become larger or make something larger
traditionally: being done in a particular way for a long time
worry (n): the feeling of being unhappy or anxious about something

In China, Your Phone Is Your Wallet

1 It's no surprise that the country that invented paper, printing, the compass, and paper money is now leading the world in cashless banking. In China, mobile payment apps are very popular. People think they're great. And they're not just a fad—here today, gone tomorrow. People like to use these apps to buy food in stores and restaurants, to pay bills and taxes, and even to tip street performers, such as musicians and singers. They also enjoy using them to schedule and pay for taxis, air and train travel, and doctor's appointments.

1. What is the main idea of Paragraph 1?
   a. Mobile payment apps are the best way to pay for purchases.
   b. Mobile payment apps are popular in China.
   c. Mobile payment apps are an easy way to pay for travel.

2 In 2017, China spent $12.8 trillion using mobile payment apps, compared to $49.3 billion spent by users in the United States. Because China is home to 1.4 billion people, it's natural that the market is much larger, yet what explains the apps' popularity among the Chinese?

2. Is this statement *T* (true) or *F* (false)?
   T / F   More money was spent in the United States using mobile payment apps than in China.

(Continued)

3 First, for a mobile payment to happen, a person must have a smartphone, and there are many in China. In 2017, around 663 million Chinese owned one. Secondly, Chinese people enjoy the convenience of mobile payments. For instance, there is no need to go to the bank to get money because it's always available on the phone. Also, traditionally, many Chinese really dislike owing money with credit cards, so mobile payments are popular because most are connected to the person's debit card. And, like all people, Chinese people want their money to be safe. Using a mobile wallet is like using cash; however, there is no worry about losing your money. In addition, for Chinese traveling abroad, it's an easy way to spend money. Instead of changing their yuan (Chinese money) to the local money, they can use their mobile wallet.

3. What is the main idea of Paragraph 3?
   a. There are many reasons why mobile payments are popular in China.
   b. Many Chinese own smartphones, and that is why mobile payment apps are popular.
   c. Mobile payment apps make it easy to travel abroad.

4 Finally, another reason for mobile payment's popularity is the availability of the service. Chinese mobile payment apps Alipay and WeChat Pay are two of the most popular, and both have expanded into other countries that are popular with tourists. For instance, currently about 70 countries accept Alipay, including Malaysia, Russia, France, the United States, and South Africa. Both companies are trying to get more stores and countries to accept their service.

4. What is the main idea of Paragraph 4?
   a. Many stores in the United States now accept Alipay.
   b. Tourists enjoy using mobile payment apps.
   c. Chinese mobile payment apps are accepted in many different countries.

5 As the popularity of mobile payments continues to grow in China, other countries will probably follow China's example. In the future, don't be surprised to see street performers in Kuala Lumpur or Kathmandu accepting tips through their smartphones.

5. Which statement best describes the main idea of the article?
   a. Many countries, such as France and the United States, accept mobile payments.
   b. Mobile payments are popular in China because many people own smartphones.
   c. China's use of mobile payments is an example for other countries to follow.

THINK ABOUT LANGUAGE

A. Combine the independent clauses to make compound sentences. Use the connectors from the box. More than one correct answer may be possible.

but	however	in addition	so	therefore

1. Many people own smartphones / Mobile payment apps are popular here

    _____

    _____

2. Many Chinese enjoy paying for goods with mobile payment apps / Large and small Chinese businesses should accept them

    _____

    _____

3. Shells were accepted as payment in the past / Now they are not accepted

    _____

    _____

4. Some stores accept cash, checks, and credit / They take mobile payments

    _____

    _____

5. Many large stores accept mobile payments / Some smaller stores accept only cash.

    _____

    _____

B. Read each sentence. Circle the correct meaning of the boldfaced word.

1. In Roman times, people **traded** salt for other goods, such as silk and spices.
    a. gave something for something else
    b. paid for something with money
    c. gave something away
    d. did a job

2. Early Chinese emperors often were **buried** with a cowry shell inside their mouth.
    a. had a ceremony for someone who has died
    b. left outside
    c. put into the ground after dying
    d. took care of someone

3. **Generation** Z (people born 1995–2012) enjoys using mobile payments.
    a. a group of children
    b. a period of time, usually 100 years
    c. all the people in a society who are about the same age
    d. a length of time, usually 50 years

4. Some people are **not so sure about** the benefits of mobile payments. They worry about the loss of privacy.
   a. unhappy about
   b. not supportive of
   c. not interested in
   d. uncertain about

5. China has a large mobile payment **market** because there are so many people who live there.
   a. a group of people who wants to buy something
   b. a place where you can buy goods
   c. a store that sells mobile phones
   d. a place that trades goods for services

🔊 Go to **MyEnglishLab** to complete grammar and vocabulary practices.

ASSIGNMENT

Think about what you have read about mobile payments. Think about your knowledge of or experience with mobile payments. Write an opinion paragraph expressing what you like or dislike about mobile payments.

PREPARE TO WRITE

A. Think about what you like and dislike about mobile payments. Make a list using the T-chart.

MOBILE PAYMENTS	
What I Like	What I Dislike

B. With a partner or in a small group, discuss the information in your T-chart. Ask questions. For example:

What do you really like (or dislike) about mobile payments?

What are problems with mobile payments?

WRITE

Write a draft paragraph that expresses your opinion about mobile payments.

- Explain what you like or dislike.
- Use three connectors to make compound sentences.

> **TIP**
>
> A paragraph is a group of about 6–10 sentences about a single topic. In academic writing, paragraphs usually have a **topic sentence** that tells the main idea. The topic sentence is often the first sentence of the paragraph. The other sentences (supporting sentences) give more information about the topic.

PROOFREAD AND EDIT

A. Read your paragraph and circle any mistakes. Answer the questions in the chart.

Did you ...	Yes	No	Notes
indent your paragraph?			
start each sentence with a capital letter?			
use correct punctuation to end each sentence?			
write about one topic?			
write about likes or dislikes?			
use connectors to combine independent clauses?			

B. Share your paragraph with a partner. Read your partner's paragraph and answer the questions in the chart.

Peer Review Form	Notes
What is the topic of the paragraph? What is the writer's opinion about that topic?	
How many sentences are there?	
Are there at least three connectors used to make compound sentences?	
Is the paragraph formatted correctly? (indented with correct capitalization and punctuation)	
Do you have any questions or comments for the writer?	

C. Discuss the feedback with your partner. Then write a second draft.

DEVELOP SOFT SKILLS

MAKING A BUDGET

By learning how to make a budget, you can better manage your money. A budget helps you control how much you spend.

A. Preview the article. What is it about?

B. Read the article.

> ### Glossary
>
> advice: a suggestion about what someone should do
> supplies: things that you need for daily life

On Budget

1 Being a student at university is expensive. For example, you have to buy books and other supplies for class. If you live away from home, you need to pay for food and a place to live. Going to school in another country can be even more expensive.

2 Making a budget is an important skill. A budget shows the money you have and your expenses—the things you plan to spend your money on. In addition to listing expenses, it's a good idea to include savings, or extra money, in your budget. Savings can be used for emergencies.

3 Take Chen, for example: Chen started each month with $1,500, but he often spent more and had to ask his friends for money. Chen decided to get some advice from Student Services about making a budget. These are the steps he learned:

    1. Write down how much money you have at the beginning of each month.

    2. Write down all of your expenses for the month.

    3. Don't spend more than your budget says.

4 Chen followed the advice and now makes a budget. The chart shows how Chen spends his money now.

CHEN'S MONTHLY BUDGET	
Starting Amount	+$1,500
Expenses	
Apartment	−$550
Phone	−$75
Car / Bus / Train	−$150
Food / Restaurants	−$375
Clothes	−$50
Fun	−$225
Savings	−$75
Total	**$1,500**

Chen's Expenses

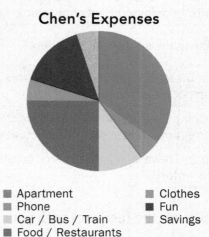

■ Apartment   ■ Clothes
■ Phone   ■ Fun
■ Car / Bus / Train   ▨ Savings
■ Food / Restaurants

C. Read each statement and circle *T* (true) or *F* (false). Correct the false statements.

T / F   1. Studying abroad is expensive.

T / F   2. Making a budget can help you manage your money.

T / F   3. It's a good idea to include savings in your budget.

T / F   4. Savings are for extra fun.

D. Discuss these questions with a partner or in a small group.

1. What expenses do you have each month? How much do you spend on each item?
2. What items could you spend less on?

E. How much money do you have each month? Make a budget. How much do you have left for savings each month? Complete the chart.

MY MONTHLY BUDGET	
Starting Amount	+$
Expenses	
Apartment	−$
Phone	−$
Car / Bus / Train	−$
Food / Restaurants	−$
Clothes	−$
Fun	−$
Savings	−$
Total	$

WHAT DID YOU LEARN?

Read the sentences. Check (✓) what you learned.

☐ I can preview to predict topics and main ideas.

☐ I can express likes and dislikes.

☐ I can use connectors in compound sentences.

☐ I can guess meaning from context.

☐ I can make a budget.

🔾 Go to **MyEnglishLab** to complete a self-assessment.

Chapter 2 A Cashless World

CHAPTER PROFILE

In this chapter, you will study another area of **money and e-commerce**: life without cash.

You will learn the answers to these questions:

• What are cashless restaurants?

• What are unstaffed stores, and why are they becoming popular?

• What is good about a cashless world? What are the problems of a cashless world?

OUTCOMES

• Scan for details
• Give examples
• Use the present perfect
• Keep a vocabulary journal
• Protect your money

For more about **MONEY AND E-COMMERCE**, see Chapter 1. See also [OC] **MONEY AND E-COMMERCE**, Chapters 1 and 2.

GETTING STARTED

Discuss these questions with a partner or in a small group.

1. Have you ever bought or sold something online? Explain.

2. Is it necessary to staff a store with workers? Or can technology do the job?

3. Look at the picture to the right. What does it show? A cashless business accepts only credit and debit cards or mobile payments, like Apple Pay or WeChat Pay. How is a cashless business good for a business owner? For a shopper?

○ Go to **MyEnglishLab** to complete a self-assessment.

READ

SKILL: SCANNING FOR DETAILS

WHY IT'S USEFUL By scanning, you can identify details and better understand the information that supports the main idea.

As you saw in Chapter 1, the main idea of a reading expresses a particular idea about a topic. **Details** give readers more information about that main idea. There are many types of details, including the following:

- **Facts** are information that can be proven and do not change from person to person—for example, names of people and places, dates, statistics.

- **Definitions** of important words are often set inside commas, dashes, or parentheses.

- **Examples** are often introduced with *for example* or *for instance*.

- **Anecdotes** are short, interesting stories about a person or event.

Scanning for details is searching a reading for specific information. Scanning can save you time. For example, when taking a test or finishing an assignment, you may need to find details quickly.

How to Scan

- Decide what details you need to find—for example, a name, a date, a specific word.

- Look for capital letters (for names of people, things), numbers (for times, dates, amounts), or specific words.

- If you are answering a question, look for clues in the question itself:

  - *Who ... ?* = person   Look for capital letters.
  - *Where ... ?* = location (cities, states, countries)   Look for capital letters.
  - *When ... ?* = time   Look for numbers or capital letters for days and months.

- Don't read each word of the reading. Instead, skim the reading.

Try scanning.

- First, read the question below the article "Mr. Amazon: Jeff Bezos." Notice what information you need to find: *when* and *where*.
- Next, read the paragraph.
- Then try to answer the question. Scan the paragraph for that information. Clue: Look for numbers and capital letters.
- Read how another student answered. Do you agree?

Mr. Amazon: Jeff Bezos

The name Jeff Bezos is famous in the e-commerce world. Bezos is the founder and chief executive officer of Amazon®, one of the world's largest e-commerce websites. Bezos started Amazon in 1994 in Seattle, Washington (USA), as an online bookstore. However, the company soon added other items, such as toys, office supplies, and clothes, and Bezos became a leader in the e-commerce world. This has made Bezos very successful in many ways. For example, as of August 2018, he was worth $151 billion, making him one of the richest people in the world. And almost everyone in the United States has bought something from his company.

When and where did Jeff Bezos start Amazon?

in 1994, in Seattle, Washington (USA)

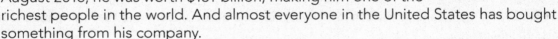

CULTURE NOTE

Charity-minded customers of Amazon can shop its other website, smile.amazon.com. A percentage of all purchases goes to charity. As of August 2018, contributions to charities totaled about $97 million.

REMEMBER

Circle all correct answers.

Details can be _____ .

a. definitions   b. anecdotes   c. facts   d. examples

VOCABULARY PREVIEW

Read the words. Circle the ones you know. Put a question mark (?) next to the ones you don't know.

account (n)	crime	focus on (v)	policy
charge (v)	fee	make sense	the poor

🔊 Go to **MyEnglishLab** to complete a vocabulary practice.

Preview the article "Cash Not Welcome Here." Then scan for numbers and names. Circle all correct answers.

1. What kinds of numbers are in the article?
   a. $ b. % (percent)   c. age

2. What names are in the article?
   a. credit card companies   b. smartphones   c. countries

3. What do you think you will read about?
   a. cashless restaurants   b. the importance of cash   c. how to start a restaurant

READ

A. Read the article. Do not stop to look up words. Answer the questions.

> Glossary
>
> cover (v): to be enough money to pay for something
> make change: to return extra money to a customer who has paid with a larger bill
> price (n): the amount of money that you pay to buy something
> purchase (n): the act of buying something
> robbery: the crime of stealing from a person
> theft: the crime of stealing something

Cash Not Welcome Here

1 At first, it looks like any other restaurant: tables and chairs, food and drinks, servers and menus. It's only when you are ready to pay that you notice the difference: no cash accepted—only cards and apps.

2 For customers, eating at a cashless restaurant may seem like a piece of cake, but there are concerns. For one, people worry that a cashless policy discriminates against—or is unfair toward—the young and the poor. For example, what if a customer doesn't have a credit card or a smartphone with the app? Most credit cards, for example, require users to be a certain age to get one—usually 18 or older. And smartphones are expensive, costing $350 or more, on average. In addition, some people, like the poor, don't have bank accounts and use only cash. Lastly, some believe cashless policies will lead to higher prices. Credit card companies charge a fee to restaurants—about 2 percent of the purchase—every time a card is used. To cover that charge, many restaurants increase their prices.

(Continued)

1. In Paragraph 2, what kind of detail is "—or is unfair toward—"?
   a. date
   b. name
   c. definition

3 For restaurant owners, however, a cashless policy makes good business sense. First, it's a time saver. For example, employees don't have to make change, count and record the money, or take it to the bank. Instead they can focus on the customer. This is important to servers in the US, for example, because they earn at least 40 percent of their income from tips. Also, a cashless policy saves owners from worrying. They don't have to think about crimes such as robbery and employee theft. Finally, it can save the restaurant money. For instance, there's no need to buy a cash register, purchase a safe, or pay for security.

2. Consider the question "In what country do servers make a lot of their money in tips?" What would you scan for and find in Paragraph 3?
   a. number / 40 percent
   b. name / US
   c. noun / restaurant

4 As more and more restaurants try the cashless model, it'll be interesting to see which side wins out. They say the customer is always right, but everyone knows that time is money and money talks.

B. Were your predictions in Predict correct?

↻ Go to **MyEnglishLab** to reread the article.

C. What does a cashless policy save owners? Scan the article.

   1. _time_ _____

   2. _____

   3. _____

CULTURE NOTE

English has many idioms, or expressions, that have a different meaning from the usual meaning of the individual words.
For instance:

Money talks: Money gives someone power and influence to get things done.

a piece of cake: easy to do

Time is money: Time is valuable, so don't waste it.

When reading, follow these steps to identify the details:

1) Read to understand the main idea.
2) Turn the main idea into a *wh-* question. For instance, if the main idea is "E-commerce is becoming popular," then ask yourself, "Why is e-commerce becoming more popular?"
3) Reread to find the answers (details).

D. Reread the article. Circle the correct answers.

1. What is the main idea of the article?
   a. Cashless restaurants are good for everyone.
   b. Cashless restaurants are good for customers, but there are concerns for owners.
   c. Cashless restaurants are good for owners, but there are concerns for customers.
   d. Cashless restaurants are a piece of cake to own.

2. What does the idiom "a piece of cake" mean?
   a. sweet and usually eaten after a meal
   b. easy to do
   c. difficult to understand
   d. concerning

3. What examples of discrimination are given in Paragraph 2? Circle TWO.
   a. Smartphones can be expensive.
   b. Credit card companies require an app.
   c. Some people don't have bank accounts.
   d. Teenagers do not have smartphones.

4. Why is the 2 percent credit card fee statistic included?
   a. to make the reading longer
   b. to show the cause of higher prices at cashless restaurants
   c. to define the word *discriminate*
   d. to explain how a cashless policy is good for the customer

5. Which detail supports the idea that a cashless policy is good for servers?
   a. Servers don't have to spend money on security guards.
   b. Servers can focus more on the customers and get better tips.
   c. Servers don't have to worry about employer theft.
   d. Servers can help more in the kitchen.

E. Discuss the questions with a partner.

1. Have you ever eaten at a cashless restaurant or would you like to eat at one? Explain.
2. Do you think cashless restaurants can be successful in your community? Explain.

F. In your everyday life, do you scan to find details? How is scanning useful? Share your ideas with a partner.

VOCABULARY REVIEW

Read each sentence. Then circle the meaning of the boldfaced word.

1. Because of the restaurant's cashless **policy**, I had to use my credit card and not cash.
   a. rule
   b. record
   c. sign
   d. paper

2. The man had an **account** where he could safely put his money.
   a. place at the bank
   b. explanation
   c. form of money
   d. person who counts money

3. Many museums **charge** visitors because the museums need money to pay for expenses.
   a. count
   b. give an order
   c. are responsible for
   d. ask for money

4. In addition to tuition costs, university students have to pay **fees** for using the library and participating in activities.
   a. bookstores
   b. time
   c. money
   d. banks

5. A cashless policy **makes sense** to business owners because there are many advantages, such as saving time and money.
   a. is based on good reasons
   b. has many views
   c. causes good feelings
   d. comes from opinions

6. If Jamal wants to do well in his class, he must **focus on** his schoolwork.
   a. work less on
   b. stay up late
   c. see clearly
   d. give full attention to

7. Usually **the poor** are the people affected the most by any changes to money.
   a. individuals who do not work
   b. citizens of a country
   c. people who have little money
   d. members of a community

8. Shoplifting—taking something from a store without paying for it—is a **crime** in many countries and can be punished by law.
   a. misunderstanding
   b. illegal action
   c. bad person
   d. small mistake

⬆ Go to **MyEnglishLab** to read another article.

WRITE

SKILL: GIVING EXAMPLES

WHY IT'S USEFUL By giving examples, you can add information that explains the topic or main idea.

In university classes, professors expect you to fully explain your ideas. **Giving examples** is one way to support and develop your ideas. Study the chart.

Introducing Examples	
Examples are often introduced by these signal words: *for instance, for example, like,* and *such as.*	
At the beginning of a sentence: Use a comma after the signal word.	Many credit card companies support cashless policies. **For instance,** in 2017 Visa® gave money to businesses that planned to go cashless.
In the middle of a sentence: Use commas around the example, including the signal word.	Cashless restaurants**, like** Sweetgreen™ in the United States**,** are becoming more common in cities.
At the end of a sentence: Use a comma before the signal word.	There are more and more cashless restaurants**,** *like* Sweetgreens in the United States. There are many popular e-commerce sites**, such as** Amazon, Jingdong™, and Rakuten™.
Between two independent clauses: Use a semicolon before the example clause, to connect the two clauses.	Cashless restaurants can be good for business owners**; for example,** owners can save money by not buying equipment like cash registers.

Read the excerpt (from "Mr. Amazon: Jeff Bezos"). Notice the boldfaced signal words and the examples they introduce. Notice the punctuation.

… The company soon added other items, **such as** toys, office supplies, and clothes, and became a leader in the e-commerce world. This has made Bezos very successful in many ways. **For example**, as of August 2018, he was worth $151 billion, making him one of the richest people in the world.

REMEMBER

Complete the sentence.

Giving examples is one way to add _____ to your topic.

TIP

Giving examples is just one way to support your ideas. Other ways include giving facts, reasons, explanations, definitions, and descriptions.

Grammar for Writing Using the present perfect

The **present perfect** is used to talk about things that happened or started in the past. It is commonly used in both written and spoken English.

The present perfect is formed with the present form of *have* + the past participle. The past participle is formed by adding *-ed* to the end of a regular verb. Irregular verbs have different forms. Study the chart. Notice the punctuation.

Life Experiences	
Use the present perfect to write about experiences.	I **have eaten** at a cashless restaurant in New York City.
Negative statements use *not* or *never* = not one time.	He **has** <u>not</u> **gone** to a cashless restaurant. He **has** <u>never</u> **gone** to a cashless restaurant.
Questions use *not* or *ever* = at any time.	**Have** you <u>ever</u> **wanted** to visit a cashless restaurant?

Repeated Past Actions	
Use the present perfect to write about things that happened more than once in the past.	I **have bought** many things online.
Time expressions include *since ...* (+ month, year, etc.) and *lately*.	<u>Since 2016,</u> he **has paid** for items using mobile payments. **Have** you **seen** a good movie <u>lately</u>?

Ongoing Events	
Use the present perfect to write about ongoing events.	We **have driven** 10 miles.
Time expressions include *for ...* + (number + months, years, etc.), *since ...* (+ month, year, etc.), and *all day*.	I **have lived** in Kuwait <u>for eight years</u>. Amazon's headquarters **have been** in Seattle, Washington, <u>since 1994</u>. **Has** she **worked** <u>all day</u>?

GRAMMAR NOTE

Unlike the present perfect, the simple past is used to describe something that happened only one time in the past or at a specific time in the past.

REMEMBER

Circle the correct answer.

Use the present perfect to describe things that happened or started in the _____ .

a. present   b. past   c. future

A. Complete each vocabulary journal entry with categories from the box.

Definition	Part of speech	Word	Word family	Word in context

1. Word: *check out* _Part of speech_ : verb
   _____ : to pay a bill and leave
   _____ : The customer **checks out** by scanning each item and paying with a mobile payment app.

2. Word: *cashier* _____ : noun
   _____ : someone whose job is to receive and pay out money in a bank, shop, etc.
   _____ : cash (n), cash (v)
   Word in context: Unstaffed stores don't have to pay for employees, such as **cashiers**.

3. _____ : convenience _____ : noun
   Definition: the quality of being useful, helpful, or easy
   _____ : convenient, inconvenient
   Word in context: Unstaffed stores are open around the clock—meaning more profit and more **convenience** for shoppers.

B. Complete the journal entries with vocabulary words from one of the articles in this chapter. Use a dictionary if necessary.

1. Word: _____ Part of speech: _____
   Definition: _____
   Word in context (from the article): _____
   Your own sentence: _____

2. Word: _____ Part of speech: _____
   Definition: _____
   Word in context (from the article) _____
   Your own sentence: _____

3. Word: _____ Part of speech: _____
   Definition: _____
   Word in context (from the article): _____
   Your own sentence: _____

TIP

You may also want to include these features in your vocabulary journal entries:
- a visual: a picture that helps explain the word
- synonyms: words with a similar meaning
- antonyms: words with the opposite meaning

C. Work with another student. Teach three of your words to each other. Record the words you learn in the journal below.

1. Word: _____ Part of speech: _____

   Definition: _____

   Your own sentence: _____

2. Word: _____ Part of speech: _____

   Definition: _____

   Your own sentence: _____

3. Word: _____ Part of speech: _____

   Definition: _____

   Your own sentence: _____

D. Think about the questions. Then share answers with a partner.

How do you currently record new words? What do you like about keeping a vocabulary journal?

APPLY YOUR SKILLS

In this chapter, you learned about cashless restaurants and unstaffed stores. Now you will read about how cashless societies may discriminate against the poor. You will also write a paragraph about your experience with cellphone technology.

BEFORE YOU READ
Discuss these questions with one or more students.

1. Are cashless businesses good for everyone? What are some of the problems of a cashless business?

2. A society is a group of people who live in the same community and follow the same laws. What do you think a cashless society is? Is a cashless society good for everyone?

VOCABULARY PREVIEW
Read the words. Circle the ones you know. Put a question mark (?) next to the ones you don't know.

accept	economy	include	upset (adj)
create	employ	order (v)	

🔊 Go to **MyEnglishLab** to complete a vocabulary practice.

READ

A. Read the question after each paragraph in the article "Cashless Societies—Good for All?" What information does it ask for?

B. Scan each paragraph for the information. Answer the questions.

Glossary

benefit (v): to be useful or helpful to someone

corruption: dishonest or immoral behavior, especially by people in power

critic: someone who says that a person or idea is bad or wrong

exchange (v): to give something to someone who gives you something else

housekeeper: someone whose job is to clean, cook, etc., in a house or hotel

laborer: someone who does hard work with his or her hands

removal: the act of taking something away from a place

tax evasion: when you avoid paying your taxes

vendor: someone who sells something, especially on the street

---

Cashless Societies—Good for All?

1 In 2016, Prime Minister Narendra Modi of India ordered the removal of the 1,000 rupee note (valued at about $14.50). Most Indians were upset and ran to the bank to exchange their money before it became useless. Modi's idea was to fight corruption and tax evasion, but the result was something else: Millions of Indians joined the digital economy.

    1. Prime Minister Narendra Modi ordered the removal of the _____ rupee note.
    a. 200   b. 1,000   c. 2,000

2 Before Modi's order, cash was the most popular way to do business in India. According to some reports, 95 percent of all business was done in cash, and 90 percent of businesses did not have credit card readers or accept mobile payments.

(Continued)

Now that has changed. Mobile payment companies have become popular. For example, Paytm™, India's biggest mobile payment company, currently has 200 million registered users and 7 million sellers who accept payment. However, some are asking if a cashless society benefits everyone in India.

2. _____ is India's biggest mobile payment company.
   a. WeChat Pay   b. Apple Pay   c. Paytm

3 Critics worry that the poor will be hurt the most. Two hundred seventy million people live below the poverty line, which is like living on $1.25 a day in the United States. Many of those work in India's informal economy as day laborers, housekeepers, drivers, and street vendors, for instance. Many cannot read or write and have always used cash. For this group, just feeding a family is difficult. Buying a smartphone is too difficult. However, because the people who employ these workers use mobile payments, owning a smartphone is becoming necessary.

3. About _____ people in India live below the poverty line.
   a. 270,000   b. 270,000,000   c. $1.25 a day

4 Some street vendors have accepted the change and are using mobile payment apps, like Paytm. But others just can't. According to a study by Counterpoint Research, more than 1 billion Indians don't have smartphones. Smartphone prices are going down, but smartphones still are not cheap. Meanwhile, the world is watching—and hopefully learning. When a government creates a cashless society, like Modi's government has, it must think about how to include the poor. Only then can a cashless society benefit everyone.

4. About _____ Indians don't have smartphones.
   a. 100,000   b. 1,000,000   c. 1,000,000,000

C. Now read the whole article. Were your predictions in Before You Read correct?

🔊 Go to **MyEnglishLab** to reread the article.

D. Reread the article. Read each statement and circle *T* (true) or *F* (false). Correct the false statements.

T / F   1. Prime Minister Narendra Modi ordered the removal of the 1,000 rupee note to fight corruption.

T / F   2. Before 2016, most Indians liked to pay with credit cards.

T / F   3. Paytm is the name of an unpopular mobile payment company in India.

DEVELOP SOFT SKILLS

PROTECTING YOUR MONEY

There are many people who want to take your money by using email and mobile apps. By understanding the ways thieves can take your money, you can protect yourself.

A. Preview the article. What is it about?

B. Read the article.

Glossary

deposit (n): money you pay toward an item you plan to buy

excited (adj): having strong feelings of happiness or pleasure; not calm

scam (n): a dishonest business deal that involves taking money from people

threat: a warning that someone will hurt you if you do not do what he or she wants

Protect Yourself and Your Money

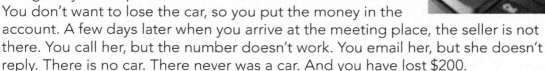

1 You just found the perfect car in an online ad. The car is beautiful and the price is low. You want to buy it. You email the seller and say you want to meet and see the car. She says that other people are interested in the car, but if you want her to hold the car for you, she needs a $200 deposit. She gives you her phone number and an account number. You don't want to lose the car, so you put the money in the account. A few days later when you arrive at the meeting place, the seller is not there. You call her, but the number doesn't work. You email her, but she doesn't reply. There is no car. There never was a car. And you have lost $200.

2 In the United States alone, online scams, like the car ad, cost people $100 billion each year. Fake ads aren't the only way scammers can get your money. Some use lies and threats. For example, some scam emails tell students that they have not paid their university fees (when, in fact, they have). Other scam emails try to look like they are from the government and say that international students must pay a fee or leave the country. These kinds of scams are illegal.

3 When we read about someone losing money to a scam, it is easy to think the person is stupid. But it's natural to be excited by a good deal or worried by a threat. In those situations, we all can make bad choices. Here are some things you can do to protect yourself and your money:

- Be smart: Never give cash in advance. Also, if a deal seems too good to be true, it probably is.

- Protect your data: Never share your bank account or credit card details with a business or person you don't trust.

- Check: If a website doesn't use "https," it is not safe. Don't use it.

- Report it: If you have been scammed or received a threatening email, tell Student Services or the police.

C. Read each statement and circle *T* (true) or *F* (false). Correct the false statements.

T / F   1. The car offer was too good to be true.

T / F   2. Online scammers lie and threaten people in hopes of getting their money.

T / F   3. Online shopping is safe if the website looks real.

T / F   4. Online scams are illegal and should be reported.

D. Discuss these questions with a partner or in a small group.

1. Have you ever lost money online? How?

2. What do you do to stay safe online?

E. Think of other ways to protect your money online. Make a list of suggestions. Share your ideas with your partner or group.

1. _____

2. _____

3. _____

WHAT DID YOU LEARN?

Read the sentences. Check (✓) what you learned.

☐ I can scan for details.

☐ I can give examples.

☐ I can use the present perfect.

☐ I can keep a vocabulary journal.

☐ I can protect my money.

🔊 Go to **MyEnglishLab** to complete a self-assessment.

🔊 Go to **MyEnglishLab** for a challenge reading about Money and E-Commerce.

Cultural Anthropology

Go to **MyEnglishLab** to watch an introduction about **HUMANITIES**.

Chapter 3 | The Power of Stories

CHAPTER PROFILE

Cultural anthropology is a field of study that looks at a group of people and their beliefs and customs. In this chapter, you will study traditional stories.

You will learn the answers to these questions:

• Why are cultural anthropologists interested in stories?

• Who is Geoffrey Chaucer, and what are *The Canterbury Tales*?

• What is *kamishibai*, and why was it important in Japanese culture?

OUTCOMES

• Recognize narratives
• Tell a story using time signals
• Use modals to express ability, possibility, and permission
• Use a dictionary to learn new words
• Understand professor feedback

For more about **CULTURAL ANTHROPOLOGY**, see Chapter 4. See also [OC] **CULTURAL ANTHROPOLOGY**, Chapters 3 and 4.

BEFORE YOU READ

Discuss these questions with one or more students.

1. Have you ever listened to a storyteller? Where did the person perform (in a school, on the street, on the radio, etc.)? Are storytellers popular in your culture?

2. To be successful, what should a good storyteller do?

VOCABULARY PREVIEW

Read the words. Circle the ones you know. Put a question mark (?) next to the ones you don't know.

festival	instead	midway	mind (v)	protect	type (n)

Ⓢ Go to MyEnglishLab to complete a vocabulary practice.

READ

A. Preview the article. What is it about?

B. Read the article. Answer the questions.

Glossary

attract: to make someone interested in something

drama: acting and plays

guarantee (v): to promise that something will happen or be done

guardian: a person who takes care of someone or something, especially a child

---

A Traditional Kamishibai Story: "Hats for Jizo"

1   *Once upon a time, there was an old man and woman who lived in a small village. They were poor and made hats to sell in town. One night before New Year's Day, the old man went into town to sell hats so he could buy supplies such as fish and rice. However, when he got there, everyone was too busy, and he couldn't sell any hats.*

    1. Why does the old man go into town?

_____

(Continued)

2 *That evening as he was walking home, it started to snow. Soon the snow covered everything, including the six statues of Jizo—a Buddhist guardian who protects people—standing just off the road. The old man stopped, brushed the snow off the statues, and put hats on their heads. But he only had five hats. "What can I use for the last statue?" he asked himself. And then he remembered his scarf. He took it off and used it to make a hat for the last statue.*

> 2. What does the old man do to the statues?
>
> _____

3 *"How was your visit to town?" the old woman asked when the man got home. He told his wife that he didn't sell any hats and what he had done with them instead. She didn't mind that he gave away the hats. Instead, the couple sat around the fire, drinking hot water, eating pickled vegetables, and singing songs about their hopes for the new year.*

> 3. How did the wife act when she found out her husband didn't sell anything?
>
> _____

4 *That night, after the couple went to bed, the old woman woke and shook the old man. "Can you hear that? It sounds like singing!" she said. When they looked outside, they saw that the Jizo statues were alive! They were singing as they walked toward the road. In front of the couple's house were food and gold coins. After that, the old couple lived happily ever after.*

> 4. Why did the Jizo statues leave food and gold at the couple's house?
>
> _____

5 Years ago, stories like "Hats for Jizo" were often told by a kamishibai performer. Kamishibai was a type of Japanese storytelling tradition. A kamishibai performer traveled from town to town on bicycle. The performer sold candy and told stories to attract and entertain the children. While telling a story, the performer would show cards with pictures of what was happening. This explains the name *kamishibai*: paper drama. To guarantee future customers, the performer would stop the story midway and continue it the next day. Kamishibai was most popular from the late 1920s to the 1950s. But then television, which was first called *denki kamishibai* (electric paper drama), came along.

As a result, many kamishibai performers turned their talents to other story types, like manga or anime. And even though kamishibai is not as popular today, there are still festivals to celebrate this traditional Japanese storytelling art.

5. How long was kamishibai popular in Japan?

_____

C. Were your predictions in Before You Read correct?

⊙ Go to **MyEnglishLab** to reread the article.

D. Reread the article. Then read each statement and circle *T* (true) or *F* (false). Correct the false statements.

T / F   1. The old couple was rich.

T / F   2. The old couple was concerned about others.

T / F   3. The old couple was sad that they had nothing good to eat.

T / F   4. The lesson of this story is that others appreciate kind acts.

T / F   5. Japanese storytellers made money by selling toys to children.

T / F   6. Kamishibai is still very popular today.

E. Complete the tasks. Discuss your ideas with a partner.

1. What are the characteristics of a narrative? Check (✓) <u>all</u> correct answers.
   ☐ It has a beginning, middle, and end.
   ☐ It informs.
   ☐ It tells a story.
   ☐ It entertains.
   ☐ It can be organized in chronological order.

2. Asking questions before, during, and after reading is a reading strategy. What other questions about this article can you ask? Think of three questions and then ask your partner.
   Who _____ ?
   What _____ ?
   Where _____ ?

VOCABULARY REVIEW

Read each sentence. Then write the correct definition of the boldfaced word.

> a particular kind of person or thing
>
> a special event
>
> between two places, and the same distance from each of them
>
> feel annoyed or angry about something
>
> in place of someone or something else
>
> prevent someone or something from being harmed or damaged

1. On Shogatsu, the New Year's Eve **festival** in Japan, people celebrate by eating soba, giving money to children, and spending time with family and friends.

   Definition: _____

2. Soba is a **type** of noodle that is long and thin. Some Japanese eat them on New Year's because they believe they are symbolic of a long and healthy life.

   Definition: _____

3. In February, Setsubun, (the Bean-Throwing Festival) is celebrated in Japan. As part of the festival, people throw beans at a person wearing a scary mask to **protect** against evil spirits.

   Definition: _____

4. **Instead** of eating soba noodles, people at Setsubun throw candy and money into crowds of people.

   Definition: _____

5. In July, **midway** through the year, Obon is another festival celebrated in Japan. This is an annual festival to remember and pay respects to family members who have died.

   Definition: _____

6. At the end of December, the emperor of Japan's birthday is a national holiday. People don't **mind** standing in the cold outside the Imperial Palace in order to get a look at the emperor.

   Definition: _____

THINK CRITICALLY

The article "A Traditional Kamishibai Story: 'Hats for Jizo'" tells a story that was commonly told by a kamishibai performer. Use information from the article to answer the questions. Then discuss your ideas with a partner.

1. Kamishibai was popular from the 1920s to the 1950s. Why do you think it is not so popular today? Where do people now get their entertainment?

   _____

   _____

2. Many stories contain a lesson that teaches a value. What is the lesson of "Hats for Jizo" and what does it say about Japanese culture?

_____

_____

THINK VISUALLY

The popularity of kamishibai decreased when television appeared. Nowadays people spend a lot of time using other electronic devices. The chart shows how much time people spend looking at screens. Use information from the chart to answer the questions. Then discuss your ideas with a partner.

Daily Screen Time (in minutes per day)					
Country	Television	Computer	Tablet	Smartphone	TOTAL
China	89	161	59	170	479
India	96	95	31	162	384
Japan	124	68	15	135	342
Russia	98	158	66	98	420
Saudi Arabia	102	99	43	189	433
South Africa	115	126	63	127	431
South Korea	127	94	14	144	379
Spain	124	97	53	122	396
Turkey	111	109	39	132	391
US	147	103	43	151	444
TOTAL	**1,133**	**1,110**	**426**	**1,430**	**4,099**

1. Which country spends the most total time looking at screens? Which one spends the least?

_____

2. Which type of screen is most popular? Which type of screen is least popular?

_____

3. How much time do you spend on screens? Which screen do you spend the most time on? Where do you fit on this chart?

_____

_____

THINK ABOUT LANGUAGE

A. Complete the sentences Use *could* or *can*.

1. In the 1930s, a kamishibai performer _____ make money by selling candy and telling stories to children.

2. Now most kamishibai performers _____ (not) make enough money because children are more interested in other forms of entertainment.

3. Eighty years ago, you _____ find kamishibai performers in the streets entertaining large groups with their stories and drawings.

4. Nowadays, here's one option for seeing a kamishibai performer: You _____ go to a kamishibai festival.

5. When I was a child, I _____ read for hours because I didn't have anything else to do.

6. Because I am in school and work, I _____ (not) read for fun, only for schoolwork.

B. *Busy* and *shake* are from the article "A Traditional Kamishibai Story: 'Hats for Jizo'." Use a dictionary to complete the charts.

busy	
Part of speech	
Pronunciation	
Other forms	
Definition	
Sentence from dictionary (if included) or article	
Your own sentence with *busy*	

shake	
Part of speech	
Pronunciation	
Other forms	
Definition	
Sentence from dictionary (if included) or article	
Your own sentence with *shake*	

⬆ Go to **MyEnglishLab** to complete grammar and vocabulary practices.

ASSIGNMENT

Think about the traditional stories you read about in this chapter. What is a traditional story that you know? It might be a fairy tale or folktale that you heard as a child. Write a paragraph explaining the story and using time signals to retell it.

PREPARE TO WRITE

A. Think about a story you know. Fill out the mind map with details.

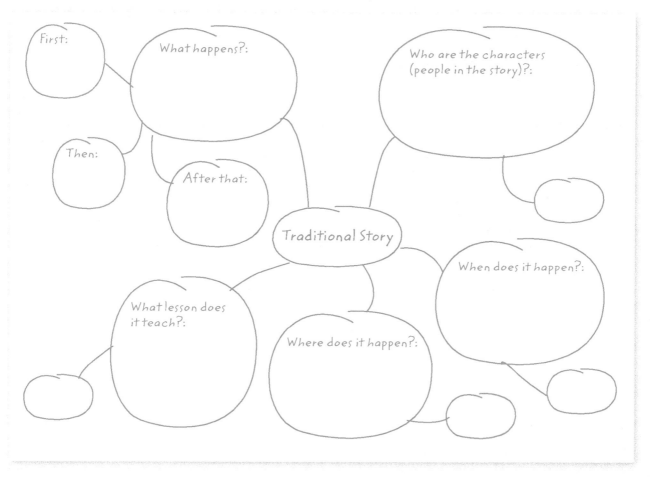

First:

What happens?:

Then:

After that:

Who are the characters (people in the story)?:

Traditional Story

What lesson does it teach?:

Where does it happen?:

When does it happen?:

B. With a partner or in a small group, discuss the information in the mind map. Ask questions. For example:

What is the story about? What do the characters look like? How old are they? How do they act?

What is the setting / where does the story happen? What time of year is it? How is the weather?

Is this story very well-known in your culture? Why do you think it's popular?

WRITE

Write a draft paragraph that tells the story.

- Use three time signals.
- Use the modals *can* and *could*.

PROOFREAD AND EDIT

A. Read your paragraph and circle any mistakes. Answer the questions in the chart.

Did you ...	Yes	No	Notes
indent your paragraph?			
start each sentence with a capital letter?			
use correct punctuation to end each sentence?			
write a story with a beginning, middle, and end?			
use three time signals?			
use the modals *can* and *could*?			

B. Share your paragraph with a partner. Read your partner's paragraph and answer the questions in the chart.

Peer Review Form	Notes
What is the story about?	
How many sentences are there?	
Are there at least three time signals?	
Does the writer use the modals *can* and *could*?	
Is the paragraph formatted correctly? (indented with correct capitalization and punctuation)	
Do you have any questions or comments for the writer?	

C. Discuss the feedback with your partner. Then write a second draft.

DEVELOP SOFT SKILLS

UNDERSTANDING PROFESSOR FEEDBACK

Professors often give students feedback through written comments and rubrics (see below). By understanding feedback, you can improve your writing.

A. Preview the article. What is it about?

B. Read the article.

> **Glossary**
>
> performance: your ability to do something well
>
> specific: saying clearly and exactly what you mean

Understanding Feedback

1 Many writing professors teach writing as a process. Usually the process is this: 1) First, the student hands in a draft of the writing assignment. 2) Then the professor gives the student feedback. 3) Next, the student uses the feedback to make changes to the assignment. 4) Finally, the student hands in a revised—rewritten and improved—draft. In order to improve your writing, it is important to understand your professor's feedback. Consider these common questions about feedback.

What is a rubric?

2 A professor may provide feedback with a rubric. A rubric is a chart with performance descriptions (for example: *Good / OK / Needs work*). Read the description for the highest category (for example, *Good*). Then see which category your writing was marked as. What is the difference? Try to make those changes in your next draft.

What do written comments mean?

3 Your professor might also provide feedback as written comments. For example, your professor might underline something and write a question mark (?) above it. This usually means that something is not clear. "SP" often means there is a spelling problem. If your professor uses codes like these, be sure you get an explanation of the codes from him or her. Most professors expect you to read their feedback and to make changes based on that feedback.

What if I don't understand the feedback?

4 If you don't understand the feedback after carefully reading it, ask your professor for help. Make a list of specific questions. For example, ask, "How can I make my ending clearer?" instead of "How can I get a better grade?" Asking specific questions shows your professor you have read the feedback and that you are trying to understand it. Then make an appointment or email your questions. Your professor will be happy to help you!

C. Read each piece of advice and circle *T* (true) or *F* (false). Correct the false advice.

T / F   1. Use feedback to help improve your writing.

T / F   2. Use the descriptions on a rubric to understand what to do.

T / F   3. Don't worry about written comments that you can't understand.

T / F   4. Think of specific questions to ask your professor before you ask for help.

D. Read Omar's paragraph. Then look at the feedback he received from his professor.

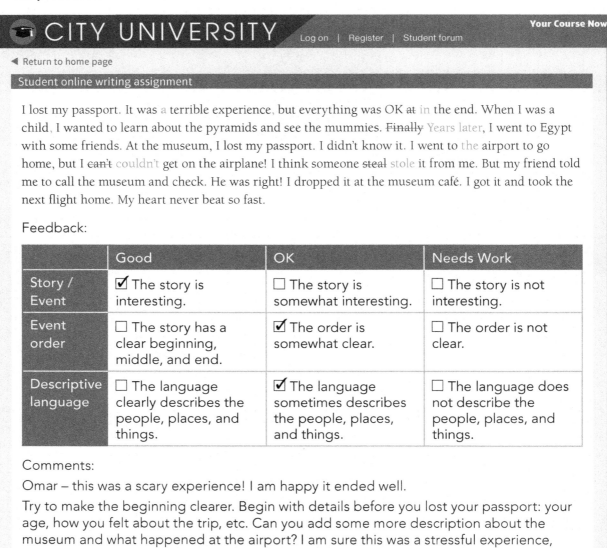

CITY UNIVERSITY

◀ Return to home page

Student online writing assignment

I lost my passport. It was a terrible experience, but everything was OK ~~at~~ in the end. When I was a child, I wanted to learn about the pyramids and see the mummies. ~~Finally~~ Years later, I went to Egypt with some friends. At the museum, I lost my passport. I didn't know it. I went to the airport to go home, but I ~~can't~~ couldn't get on the airplane! I think someone ~~steal~~ stole it from me. But my friend told me to call the museum and check. He was right! I dropped it at the museum café. I got it and took the next flight home. My heart never beat so fast.

Feedback:

	Good	OK	Needs Work
Story / Event	☑ The story is interesting.	☐ The story is somewhat interesting.	☐ The story is not interesting.
Event order	☐ The story has a clear beginning, middle, and end.	☑ The order is somewhat clear.	☐ The order is not clear.
Descriptive language	☐ The language clearly describes the people, places, and things.	☑ The language sometimes describes the people, places, and things.	☐ The language does not describe the people, places, and things.

Comments:

Omar – this was a scary experience! I am happy it ended well.

Try to make the beginning clearer. Begin with details before you lost your passport: your age, how you felt about the trip, etc. Can you add some more description about the museum and what happened at the airport? I am sure this was a stressful experience, as you describe with "my heart never beat so fast." More description will also help your readers feel what you felt.

E. With a partner, write a conversation between Omar and his professor about the feedback. Then role-play.

OMAR: _____

PROFESSOR: _____

OMAR: _____

PROFESSOR: _____

OMAR: _____

PROFESSOR: _____

F. Read feedback from one of your own assignments. Write three specific questions you could ask to get more help.

1. _____

2. _____

3. _____

TIP

Try to learn your professor's handwriting. If you can't read it, ask a friend for help. If you still can't read it, ask your professor.

WHAT DID YOU LEARN?

Read the sentences. Check (✓) what you learned.

☐ I can recognize narratives.

☐ I can tell a story using time signals.

☐ I can use modals to express ability, possibility, and permission.

☐ I can use a dictionary to learn new words.

☐ I can understand professor feedback.

◐ Go to **MyEnglishLab** to complete a self-assessment.

Chapter 4 — Storytelling Around the World

CHAPTER PROFILE

In this chapter, you will study another area of **cultural anthropology:** traditions of storytelling around the world.

You will learn the answers to these questions:

- What are shadow puppets?

- How can dance tell a story?

- What is digital storytelling, and how can it cause social change?

OUTCOMES

- Understand cause and effect
- Use descriptive language
- Describe cause-and-effect relationships
- Identify collocations
- Communicate with your professors

For more about **CULTURAL ANTHROPOLOGY**, see Chapter 3. See also [OC] **CULTURAL ANTHROPOLOGY**, Chapters 3 and 4.

2. Shadow puppets began in the 9ᵗʰ **century** in Indonesia.

Definition: _____

3. The last emperor to **lead** China was Emperor Puyi. He was only six years old when he gave up his throne in 1912.

Definition: _____

4. Some **religious** groups used shadow puppets to help teach people about their religion.

Definition: _____

5. Shadow plays used to be a **favorite** form of entertainment in China, but now movies are more popular.

Definition: _____

6. After a shadow play, the puppet master will **appear** from behind the curtain.

Definition: _____

⬆ Go to **MyEnglishLab** to read another article.

WRITE

SKILL: USING DESCRIPTIVE LANGUAGE

WHY IT'S USEFUL By using descriptive language, you can help the reader "see" the people, places, and things in your writing.

When giving an explanation, you may need to describe something in more detail. Details give additional information and add support to your ideas. **Using descriptive language** will help "catch" the reader's attention and make it easier for the person to visualize the story.

The chart shows the kinds of descriptions that you can include when writing about people, places, and things.

DESCRIPTIVE LANGUAGE		
Description of	**Kind of Description**	
People	Identification Physical qualities Feelings (likes / dislikes)	The woman was a **storyteller**. She was **small**, but she had a **big voice** and **moved with energy**. She **loved** to tell stories.
Places	Location Sights / Colors Sounds	She performed in a **busy** park in the **center of the city**. The **horns** of cars and **shouts** of kids playing filled the air.
Things	Size / Shape Color Texture	We sat at **large wooden** picnic table under a **shady** oak tree and listened to her story.

Read the student paragraph. Notice these annotations: <u>Person</u>   Place   **Thing**

| File | **Home** | Insert | Page layout | Object | Type | View | Window | Help |

Ammad the Storyteller

Where I grew up, there was a <u>storyteller named Ammad</u>. He was <u>old</u> and <u>short</u>. His <u>long, white</u> beard <u>touched the floor</u> when he sat. He looked almost <u>90</u> but <u>moved</u> <u>like a young man</u>. Ammad <u>loved to tell stories</u> and was <u>famous</u> around town. Every Friday night, he came to the local coffeehouse and entertained customers. It was a small room with eight **round tables**. Its **red walls** had turned **brown** with time, and **thick curtains** hung over the tall windows. It was noisy with talking and laughter, but became quiet when Ammad began his story.

REMEMBER

Circle <u>all</u> correct answers.

Descriptive language helps add _____ to your writing.

a. more information

b. details

c. interest

Grammar for Writing Describing cause-and-effect relationships

By using **cause and effect** expressions, you can **describe the relationship** between events. Many university-level writing assignments ask students to explain **what** happened and **why**. Words like *because* and *since* introduce the cause (the reason). Words like *so* and *as a result* introduce the effect (the result). Study the chart. Notice the punctuation.

Cause (Reason)	
because + noun + verb	**Because** <u>they were entertaining</u>, shadow plays were popular.
because of + noun	**Because of** <u>their popularity</u>, shadow plays were sometimes performed at weddings.
since + noun + verb	Shadow plays are not as popular today **since** <u>we now have many other ways to tell stories</u>.
now that + noun + verb	**Now that** <u>many Chinese have Internet,</u> **they do not watch as many shadow plays.**
when + noun + verb	**When** <u>the puppet master got sick,</u> the shadow play was canceled.

3. Conspiracy for Good is an example of a(n) _____ that uses digital storytelling.
   a. easy game
   b. board game
   c. virtual game
   d. online game

4. Because of the donations that players made, 50 girls received _____ .
   a. 10 libraries
   b. 10,000 games
   c. educational scholarships
   d. food

5. The author uses the example of Natalia to show the positive effect of including _____ on websites.
   a. opinions
   b. personal narratives
   c. numbers
   d. children

6. Because of donations, Charity: Water has funded about _____ water projects.
   a. 280
   b. 2,820
   c. 28,200
   d. 282,000

E. Answer the questions. Discuss your ideas with a partner.

1. How can a good reader understand reasons and results? Circle your ideas.
   a. look for cause signals (*because, because of, the cause of …*)
   b. guess meaning from context
   c. ask questions, such as "Why did that happen?" What was the result of x?"
   d. look for effect signals (*so, as a result, therefore*)
   e. look for time signals

2. Asking questions is one strategy for understanding cause and effect. What questions can you ask about "How Digital Storytelling Can Change Lives"? Think of three questions and then ask your partner.

   Why _____ ?

   What _____ ?

   How _____ ?

VOCABULARY REVIEW

Complete the sentences. Use the words from the box. Use the correct form.

connect	event	receive	solve	support	take part

1. Many charity organizations will organize a(n) _____ , such as a race or a dance, to raise money.

2. The charity will _____ money from people who participate in those events.

3. I give money to the local radio station to _____ its programming and workers.

4. Some people prefer not to _____ in an event, but to just give money to the charity.

5. Some charities will _____ the person giving the money to the person receiving the help. They might encourage the two to contact each other.

6. Giving money to a charity might not _____ all the world's problems, but it can help to make a difference in someone's life.

THINK CRITICALLY

The article "How Digital Storytelling Can Change Lives" explains how organizations use digital storytelling for social change. Use information from the article to answer the questions. Then discuss your ideas with a partner.

1. Conspiracy for Good is an online game that gives players a puzzle to solve. It also encourages players to donate to charities mentioned in the story. Is this common in most online games today? Do online games usually tell a story or lead to social change? What does this tell you about the creators of this game?

   _____

   _____

   _____

2. Charity: Water has funded more than 28,200 water projects around the world. What does this tell you about the availability of clean water in the world? How can having clean water change someone's life?

   _____

   _____

   _____

Tips

4 The chart includes some tips to help you communicate with your professors:

	Do	Don't
	Check the course guide for the professor's title, name, and contact information, including office location and hours.	Don't be shy. If your professor offers office hours, that's a good time to talk to him or her one-on-one. In-person communication can be clearer than email or text.
If messaging		
Subject line	Be specific. For example, write "Missed Class – ENG 107"	Don't write: "Hello" or "Our class."
Greeting	If you don't know your professor's title or name, use "Professor."	
Message	Match your professor: formal or informal language. If not sure, use formal language. Write your full name. Say which class you are in. Be short and clear about why you are writing. Apologize if you were late, missed class, or didn't hand an assignment in on time.	Don't expect your professor to know who you are. Never ask, "Did I miss anything important?" Professors believe all their classes are important!
Closing	Thank the professor for his or her time. Check your spelling and punctuation.	

5 Students want to learn and need professors to help them. Showing respect and communicating clearly is the first step toward that goal.

C. Circle <u>all</u> correct answers.

1. Use first names with _____ if they say it is OK.
   a. TAs
   b. lecturers
   c. professors

2. Office hours are _____ .
   a. when the professor meets with other professors
   b. a time for students to talk to the professor
   c. weekdays, 9–5

3. When messaging your professor, always _____ .
   a. include a clear subject line
   b. write your full name and class
   c. apologize

4. Before you send the message, be sure to _____ .
   a. write a final paragraph summarizing your ideas
   b. check the spelling
   c. fix punctuation errors

D. Read the email from Alejandro to his professor, explaining why he missed class. With a partner, find, discuss, and correct the errors.

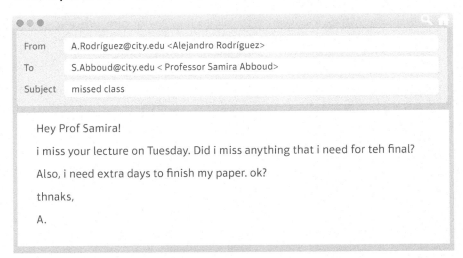

From	A.Rodríguez@city.edu <Alejandro Rodríguez>
To	S.Abboud@city.edu < Professor Samira Abboud>
Subject	missed class

Hey Prof Samira!

i miss your lecture on Tuesday. Did i miss anything that i need for teh final?

Also, i need extra days to finish my paper. ok?

thnaks,

A.

E. Draft an email to a professor about an issue you have been wanting to discuss. Share drafts with a partner and give feedback.

WHAT DID YOU LEARN?

Read the sentences. Check (✓) what you learned.

☐ I can understand cause and effect.

☐ I can use descriptive language.

☐ I can describe cause-and-effect relationships.

☐ I can identify collocations.

☐ I can communicate with my professors.

⊙ Go to **MyEnglishLab** to complete a self-assessment.

⊙ Go to **MyEnglishLab** for a challenge reading about Cultural Anthropology.

Civil Engineering

➤ Go to **MyEnglishLab** to watch an introduction about **STRUCTURAL SCIENCE**.

Chapter 5   Marvels in Engineering

CHAPTER PROFILE

Civil engineering is an area of study that involves the creation of structures, such as buildings, bridges, and tunnels. In this chapter, you will examine several marvels (amazing accomplishments) in engineering.

You will learn the answers to these questions:

- Who are the Maya, and why are they considered great engineers?

- Who was Emily Warren Roebling, and what was her connection to the Brooklyn Bridge?

- What is the Chunnel, and why is it a famous civil engineering project?

OUTCOMES

- Understand visuals
- Use spatial order to describe visuals
- Use adverbs of frequency
- Build word families with suffixes
- Give presentations

For more about **CIVIL ENGINEERING**, see Chapter 6. See also [OC] **CIVIL ENGINEERING**, Chapters 5 and 6.

READ

A. Preview the article. What is it about?

B. Read the article. Answer the questions.

Glossary

additional: more than you already have or more than was agreed or expected

cement (n): a powder that becomes hard like stone when mixed with water and is used in building or making sidewalks

estimated (adj): based on a rough calculation

fund (v): to provide money for a project

invasion: the act of an army attacking and entering a country or place

The Channel Tunnel: An International Engineering Marvel

1 Before 1994, if you wanted to go from France to England, you could make the 34-kilometer (21-mi.) trip across the English Channel by ferry or plane—or by swimming, if you enjoy adventure! For centuries, both the British and the French had thought about connecting the two

countries with an underground tunnel. But fear of invasion and funding problems always stopped its construction. This changed in 1985 when the leaders of both countries had a contest to find a company that could plan, fund, and build a tunnel that would stretch the distance between the two countries.

1. What information is in Paragraph 1 but not on the map?
   a. the name of the countries
   b. Dover, the name of the city in England
   c. a label to show the English Channel
   d. Calais, the name of the city in France

2 The engineering company Transmanche Link developed the winning plan. It planned for the construction of three tunnels, built next to each other. The northern tunnel was designed to bring people from England to France. The southern tunnel was to go from France to England. And an additional service tunnel—to be rarely used, only in case of an emergency—was to go in the middle. The estimated cost was $3.6 billion. Once the plan was approved, digging started from each side of the Channel.

(Continued)

TIMELINE OF THE CHANNEL TUNNEL

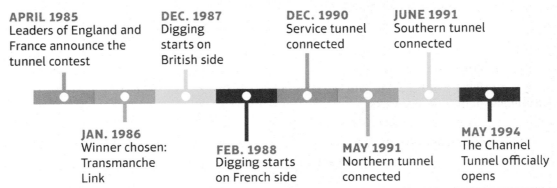

APRIL 1985
Leaders of England and France announce the tunnel contest

DEC. 1987
Digging starts on British side

DEC. 1990
Service tunnel connected

JUNE 1991
Southern tunnel connected

JAN. 1986
Winner chosen: Transmanche Link

FEB. 1988
Digging starts on French side

MAY 1991
Northern tunnel connected

MAY 1994
The Channel Tunnel officially opens

2. What was the middle tunnel to be used for?
   a. trains going from France to England
   b. trains going from England to France
   c. storage of extra materials
   d. emergencies

3. According to the timeline, when was that tunnel completed?
   a. December 1990
   b. May 1991
   c. June 1991
   d. May 1994

3 With the help of powerful tunnel boring machines, thousands of workers started digging below the ground. The dirt was moved to above ground before the cement was poured for the tunnel. Even with advanced technology, the work was often difficult. However, with the help of about 15,000 workers, the two sides met in December 1990, and the service tunnel was completed. However, workers never enjoyed a break because two more tunnels remained. The two sides finished the  northern tunnel the following year and the southern tunnel a month after that. The digging was done, but then train tracks, electrical equipment, and train stations were needed. Finally, in May 1994, the Channel Tunnel opened. After ten years, $15 billion, and the deaths of ten workers, it was finally finished.

4. What information is in the timeline *and* Paragraph 3? Circle TWO answers.
   a. the month and year the service tunnel was completed
   b. the month and year the southern tunnel was completed
   c. the month and year the Channel Tunnel was opened
   d. the month and year the northern tunnel was completed

WRITE

Write a draft paragraph that describes the particular place from your trip.

- Use spatial order.
- Use adverbs of frequency.

PROOFREAD AND EDIT

A. Read your paragraph and circle any mistakes. Answer the questions in the chart.

Did you ...	Yes	No	Notes
indent your paragraph?			
start each sentence with a capital letter?			
use correct punctuation to end each sentence?			
describe one particular place?			
use spatial order and expressions?			
use adverbs of frequency?			

B. Share your paragraph with a partner. Read your partner's paragraph and answer the questions in the chart.

Peer Review Form	Notes
What is the paragraph about?	
How many sentences are there?	
Did the writer use spatial order and expressions?	
Are there some adverbs of frequency?	
Is the paragraph formatted correctly? (indented with correct capitalization and punctuation)	
Do you have any questions or comments for the writer?	

C. Discuss your feedback with a partner. Then write a second draft.

DEVELOP SOFT SKILLS

GIVING PRESENTATIONS

A **presentation** is a talk you give about a topic to a group of people. Many university courses require students to give presentations. They can be easy if you use the right presentation tools and effective visuals.

A. Preview the article. What is it about?

B. Read the article.

Glossary

audience: the people watching a presentation
decoration: an attractive thing that is added to something to improve its appearance
design (n): a pattern
slide (n): a visual that is shown on a screen

Keys to a Successful Slide Presentation

1 In addition to knowing your topic well and practicing, there are two keys to a successful presentation: 1) Using the right presentation tools and 2) knowing what visuals or words to show on your slides. Like a good piece of writing, a good presentation takes time and effort to create. The main difference is that your presentation should use the best tools for the situation and slides with clear visuals with few words.

Tools

2 Most presentation apps, like PowerPoint®, Prezi®, Keynote®, and Google Slides™ provide you with templates. These are slides that are already made for you. You can add information to these slides for your presentation. It is best to choose a simple slide design, with a light color and not a lot of decoration.

3 There are some other things to remember about apps:

- Assignments usually say which app to use, so check.
- Be sure that your app works in the room where you will present.
- Don't use too many animation features.

Slides: Visuals + Words

4 A good rule to remember about slides is that "less is more." This means that your slides should not contain a lot of words. Aim to have only one main idea on each slide. Choose your words carefully. Do not use full sentences.

5 Try to find visuals that *show* what you want to say, like a flowchart, a photograph, a timeline, or a diagram. People remember visuals much more than they remember written words.

6 Finally, as you present, refer to notecards or your presentation app. This way, your audience can focus on your slides, and you can tell them additional information, like examples.

TIP

At the university level, presentations are often formal, with a time limit and a grade.

C. **Read the article again. Then read each statement and circle *T* (true) or *F* (false). Correct the false statements.**

T / F   1. Making a good presentation can take as much time as writing a good paper.

T / F   2. The keys to a good presentation are using the right tools and creating clear slides.

T / F   3. You should write everything you need to say on your slides.

T / F   4. You should use visuals to help people remember your presentation.

D. **Discuss these questions with a partner or in a small group.**

Which slide is the best? Why? What problems do the other two slides have? Explain.

Slide A

Slide B

Maya Pyramids
Slide C

E. **Use the paragraph that you wrote on page 124 or page 135. Create five slides using a presentation app or other technology. Follow the advice from "Keys to a Successful Slide Presentation" on page 136. Share your presentation with your partner or group.**

WHAT DID YOU LEARN?

Read the sentences. Check (✓) what you learned.

☐ I can understand visuals.

☐ I can use spatial order to describe visuals.

☐ I can use adverbs of frequency.

☐ I can build word families with suffixes.

☐ I can give a presentation.

🔊 Go to **MyEnglishLab** to complete a self-assessment.

Chapter 6 | Engineering a Better World

CHAPTER PROFILE

In this chapter, you will learn about another area of **civil engineering**: how engineers can help make the world better.

You will learn the answers to these questions:

• How can engineers help refugees?

• How can engineers build earthquake-resistant buildings?

• What is sustainable engineering, and how is it connected to the Olympic Games?

OUTCOMES

• Follow a process
• Describe a process
• Use the comparative form of adjectives
• Build word families with prefixes
• Work in groups

For more about **CIVIL ENGINEERING**, see Chapter 5. See also [OC] **CIVIL ENGINEERING**, Chapters 5 and 6.

B. Share your paragraph with a partner. Read your partner's paragraph and answer the questions in the chart.

Peer Review Form	Notes
What is the paragraph about?	
How many sentences are there?	
Did the writer explain an instructional process?	
Did the writer use sequence words?	
Did the writer use comparative adjectives?	
Is the paragraph formatted correctly? (indented with correct capitalization and punctuation)	
Do you have any questions or comments for the writer?	

C. Discuss the feedback with your partner. Ask questions about your partner's paragraph.

How do you know so much about this process?

Is the process easy or difficult to understand?

What are the benefits of knowing about this process?

D. Discuss these questions with a partner or in a small group.

Why is it important to use sequence words when describing a process? Why is it important to think about your audience (who will be reading your writing)?

VOCABULARY STRATEGY

BUILDING WORD FAMILIES WITH PREFIXES

WHY IT'S USEFUL By recognizing prefixes, you can figure out the meaning of new words.

As you saw in Chapter 5, a **word family** is a group of words with the same root. For example, the word *agree* has these "family members": *agreement, agreeable, disagree*. One way to build a word family is by adding a prefix to the beginning of a word in the family. This creates new words with different parts of speech (nouns, verbs, adjectives, adverbs) and different meanings.

Knowing the meaning of **prefixes** can help you to figure out the meaning of new words. Not all prefixes can be added to all words, so it's important to learn the most common ones. Study the chart.

Prefix	Meaning	Prefix + Word	Part of Speech
dis-	not / opposite of	**dis**agree	verb
		disappear	verb
		discomfort	noun
il-	not	**il**legal	adjective
im-		**im**possible	adjective
in-		**in**complete	adjective
mis-	wrongly	**mis**understood	adjective
		misinterpret	verb
re-	again	**re**do	verb
		regain	verb
		return	verb
un-	not	**un**do	verb
		unfriendly	adjective
		unacceptable	adjective
		unhappy	adjective

A. Make new words using the prefixes from the box. More than one correct answer may be possible. Use a dictionary if necessary.

dis-	im-	in-	mis-	re-	un-

1. _____ like

2. _____ polite

3. _____ convenient

4. _____ move

5. _____ common

6. _____ appear

7. _____ view

8. _____ believable

9. _____ behave

10. _____ patient

B. Read each sentence. Then match the definitions with the boldfaced words.

_____ 1. The building was made out of **inappropriate** materials, so it was destroyed during the earthquake.

_____ 2. Some people **disapprove** of building in areas where earthquakes occur.

_____ 3. After a severe earthquake, many people **react** by giving money as a way to help.

_____ 4. Some people are **impatient** and want to rebuild immediately after an earthquake.

_____ 5. Many people who live through a serious earthquake will **replace** their house with a structure that is more earthquake-resistant.

a. annoyed because you want something to happen now so you don't have to wait

b. not suitable or correct for a particular purpose

c. to behave in a particular way because of what someone has said or done to you

d. to think that someone or something is bad or wrong

e. to use a new or different thing

C. Circle the prefix of each word. Then complete the chart.

	Word	Meaning of Prefix	Meaning of Word	New Word with Prefix	Meaning of New Word
1.	impossible	not	not able to be done, happen, or exist		
2.	disappear				
3.	rebuild				

D. Work with another student. Follow the steps.

1. Search the chapter for words with prefixes. Make a list. Then discuss how you can use the prefix to figure out the word's meaning. For example:

    Incomplete. The prefix _in-_ means "not" and the word _complete_ means "done or finished." So _incomplete_ means "not finished."

2. How can understanding prefixes help you in your studies?

APPLY YOUR SKILLS

In this chapter, you learned how civil engineers help people. In Apply Your Skills, you will read how civil engineers are using sustainable building practices to help the world. You will also write an instructional paragraph describing a process.

BEFORE YOU READ
Discuss these questions with one or more students.

1. Sustainable building—also known as green building—is when engineers design and build a structure that is environmentally friendly. In other words, it doesn't hurt the environment. What are some things you can do to be more environmentally friendly or green?

2. The Olympics are a worldwide sporting event held every four years in a different host country. What structures do host countries need to build to prepare for the Olympics?

VOCABULARY PREVIEW
Read the words. Circle the ones you know. Put a question mark (?) next to the ones you don't know.

| athlete | compete | recycle | stadium | the environment | transportation |

◐ Go to **MyEnglishLab** to complete a vocabulary practice.

READ
A. Preview the article "How the Olympics Are Going Green" on the next page. What is it about?

B. Read the article. Answer the questions.

> Glossary
>
> atmosphere: the air that surrounds the Earth
>
> emissions: a gas or other substance that is sent into the air
>
> fuel-efficient: burning fuel in a more efficient way so that less is used
>
> harm (v): to hurt someone or something
>
> Paralympic Games: an international sports event held every 4 years for disabled athletes
>
> precious metals: a rare and valuable metal such as gold or silver
>
> promote: to help something develop and be successful

How the Olympics Are Going Green

1 When athletes compete in the 2020 Olympics in Japan, they will compete in stadiums designed and built according to sustainable engineering practices. Their medals will be made from precious metals repurposed from electronic goods like smartphones. They will use public transportation or fuel-efficient cars to travel in and around Tokyo. At night, they will sleep in athlete villages where the lumber, which was donated, will later be reused for other projects. In fact, a goal of the organizing committee is that 99 percent of all goods bought and used for the 2020 games will be reused or recycled.

1. How are the 2020 Olympics trying to "go green"?

   _____

2 For the 2020 Olympic Games, some new buildings had to be constructed, like the new stadium. But unlike past Olympics, this time engineers had to follow a certain process when designing and planning those buildings. The first step was to read and understand the Tokyo 2020 Olympic and Paralympic Games Sustainability Plan. This plan explained the sustainable rules, goals, and measures that had to be followed. When that step was finished, the engineers came up with a sustainable design for the stadium. In order to be sustainable, materials had to come from places where there was a lot of each material and where its removal would not be a disadvantage to that environment. Once sustainable materials were located, engineers had to think about how those materials would be brought to the building site. A long trip by train or truck causes more carbon dioxide emissions to go into the atmosphere, which is a factor in global warming. After finding the best way to deliver materials, they needed to construct buildings that used renewable energy (energy that is easy to replace) and could be used for future generations. The final step was to report back to the organizing committee on how the design and construction did not harm the environment.

2. What are the five steps for constructing a sustainable building for the 2020 Olympics?

   Step 1: _____

   Step 2: _____

   Step 3: _____

   Step 4: _____

   Step 5: _____

(Continued)

3 Engineers who use sustainable engineering practices know their actions can have a positive impact on the environment. The organizing committee hopes that future Olympic Games will follow the 2020 Olympics model and promote more sustainable engineering. The health of future Olympic athletes, as well as the planet, depends on it.

3. How can the Olympics help the environment?

_____

_____

Going to the 2020 Olympics? Here are some tips:

- Learn some Japanese. Download a multilingual app so you can communicate with everyone.

- Once at the Olympics, talk with a robot helper, who will give you tips on where to go, what to eat, and how to get where you want to go.

- Buy tickets for an event at the new national stadium.

- Cheer on the athletes!

C. Was your prediction in Before You Read correct?

◐ Go to MyEnglishLab to reread the article.

D. Reread the article. Circle the correct answers.

1. The Olympic organizing committee is concerned about the planet and is promoting _____ engineering practices.
   a. sustainable   b. sports   c. serious   d. suspicious

2. Using the precious metals from smartphones and turning them into medals is an example of _____ .
   a. rebuilding   b. recycling   c. being cheap   d. being careless

3. The Tokyo 2020 Olympic and Paralympic Games Sustainability Plan explains the sustainable _____ that must be followed by any engineering or building company.
   a. law   b. power   c. leaders   d. rules

4. The author mentions carbon dioxide emissions and global warming to explain the importance of what step?
   a. designing a sustainable building   b. finding sustainable materials   c. looking for the best way to deliver materials   d. building an energy-efficient structure

5. The purpose of the article is _____ .

a. to explain the history of the Olympic Games

b. to show the importance of sporting events

c. to explain how the Olympics can be a sustainable project

d. to discuss the causes of global warming

E. Complete the tasks. Discuss your ideas with a partner.

1. What should a good reader do to understand processes? Circle <u>all</u> correct answers.

a. look for sequence words (*first, then, finally* …)

b. look for imperatives (instructional)

c. ask questions such as "How did that happen?" or "How can I do that?"

d. look for flowcharts, timelines, and lists

2. When describing an informational process, the third person (*he, she, it, they*) is used, but when giving instructions, imperatives are more common. Imperatives are a little less formal. Why are imperatives more appropriate for instructional processes?

_____

VOCABULARY REVIEW

Complete the sentences. Use the words from the box. Use the correct form.

athlete	compete	recycle	stadium	the environment	transportation

1. The Olympics are an international sporting event where _____ from around the world participate.

2. Every four years, athletes _____ with the hopes of bringing home the gold medal.

3. Many host cities spend large amounts of money to build new _____ for the events.

4. Because so many people attend the Olympic Games, host cities will also have to spend a lot of money to improve their _____ systems so that everyone can get around easily.

5. Although the Olympics are a sporting event, the organizing committee is using the Olympics to highlight _____ and being responsible users of Earth's resources.

6. Everyone can help create a healthy environment and sustainability by practicing the three Rs: reduce, reuse, and _____ .

THINK CRITICALLY

The article "How the Olympics Are Going Green" explains how sustainable building practices can help the planet. Use information from the article to answer the questions. Then discuss your ideas with a partner.

1. A goal of the Olympics is to create a better, more peaceful world through sports. How can international sporting events such as the Olympics promote more than cooperation between countries?

   _____

   _____

2. The organizers of the 2020 Olympic Games worked closely with the United Nations to promote the idea of sustainability. Do you think that future Olympic host cities should follow Tokyo's sustainability plan? Explain.

   _____

   _____

THINK VISUALLY

In 2016, 1.5 billion cellphones were sold worldwide. Because most people buy new phones every few years, many of the old phones turn into electronic waste (e-waste). E-waste is electronics such as phones, computers, or other devices that are thrown away or recycled. The chart shows what happens to your phone when it is recycled. Use information from the chart to answer the questions on the next page. Then discuss your ideas with a partner.

Recycling Process of Cellphones

Consumer drops old phone in e-waste recycling container.

Recycling container brought to e-waste recycling center.

Company tests phone to see if it can be reused.

If phone can be fixed, then it is cleaned of all personal information, repaired, and sold.

If phone can't be reused, then it goes to the recycling area.

The phone is broken down into its different materials: plastic, metals, glass.

These materials are shredded (broken into very small pieces).

Materials are sent to other companies and made into new products.

Consumer buys new phone.

1. What is the first step of recycling a phone?

   _____

   _____

2. If an old phone can still be used, what happens to it?

   _____

   _____

3. Why should phones be recycled?

   _____

   _____

THINK ABOUT LANGUAGE

A. Complete the sentences. Use the comparative form of the boldfaced adjectives.

1. Sustainable engineering has become more popular in recent years as the climate has become _____ (**warm**) than ever.

2. In fact, most universities now offer sustainable engineering classes that are often _____ (**popular**) than other engineering classes.

3. Students learn how to make buildings _____ (**green**)—or, in other words, more energy efficient.

4. At first, it may be _____ (**expensive**) to build a green home. But in the long run, homeowners will save money because they will pay less for energy.

5. It's important for everyone to go green. If we don't, it will be _____ (**difficult**) to fix the problems caused by global warming.

B. Make new words using the prefixes from the box. Write sentences about "going green" using the new words.

dis-	in-	re-	un-

1. _____ turn

   Sentence: _____

2. _____ correct

   Sentence: _____

3. _____ agree

   Sentence: _____

4. _____ read

   Sentence: _____

5. _____ healthy

   Sentence: _____

⬆ Go to **MyEnglishLab** to complete grammar and vocabulary practices.

ASSIGNMENT

Think about the different processes you have read about in this chapter. What is a process you know a lot about? Choose a process and tell how to do it in an instructional paragraph.

PREPARE TO WRITE

A. Choose and circle a topic from the box or use your own idea. Then use the chart to brainstorm questions and answers.

How to become a good athlete	How to make something
How to choose a major	How to plan a great party
How to make friends	_____

Q:	A:
Q:	A:
Q:	A:
Q:	A:
Q:	A:

B. With a partner or in a small group, discuss your notes. Ask questions. For example:

Why did you choose this topic?

Why is this an important process to explain?

How did you learn to do this?

WRITE

Write a draft paragraph that explains your process.

- Use sequence words to describe the process.

- Use comparative adjectives.

PROOFREAD AND EDIT

A. Read your paragraph and circle any mistakes that you see. Answer the questions in the chart.

Did you ...	Yes	No	Notes
indent your paragraph?			
start each sentence with a capital letter?			
use correct punctuation to end each sentence?			
write about an instructional process?			
use sequence words?			
use comparative adjectives?			

B. Share your paragraph with a partner. Read your partner's paragraph and answer the questions in the chart.

Peer Review Form	Notes
What is the paragraph about?	
How many sentences are there?	
Did the writer use sequence words when describing a process?	
Are there comparative adjectives?	
Is the paragraph formatted correctly? (indented with correct capitalization and punctuation)	
Do you have any questions or comments for the writer?	

C. Discuss your feedback with a partner. Then write a second draft.

➲ Go to **MyEnglishLab** to read another article.

DEVELOP SOFT SKILLS

WORKING IN GROUPS

Knowing how to **work in groups** is important for many reasons. Group work is common in university classes. It is a regular part of working life, and your grades may depend on how well you work in groups. The sooner you learn how to work well in groups, the better!

A. Preview the article. What is it about?

B. Read the article.

Glossary

awkward: making you feel uncomfortable or embarrassed

collaborate: to work together to produce or achieve something

force (v): to make someone do something that he or she does not want to do

Experiences in Group Work

Jin-soo

1 Group work is a lot more common in college than I expected. In high school, I didn't collaborate much with others. So at first, I got nervous whenever I had to participate in a group in college. I am a little shy around new people. I have to force myself to communicate with people I don't know. But I got used to working with classmates and even made some friends.

2 I really like working in groups in class, especially in my civil engineering class. If I'm confused about something, other students can sometimes understand why better than the professor can. When my classmates explain something, I can usually understand it easily. But group work outside of class can be challenging. The main problem is scheduling. It can be hard to find a time when everyone is free. The larger the group, the bigger the problem.

Adela

3 In high school, I did some group work, but it was almost always online. So when I started college, it took a little while to understand how to work with others face-to-face. Everyone was quiet, and it was awkward. But we quickly adapted because the professors kept using it.

4 I learn a lot about other people's points of view when I am collaborating with my classmates. These are students from all over the world. We each bring different experiences and ideas. But working together isn't always easy. Everyone has an opinion about how to work together, so we have to be open. Also, I sometimes feel like I do more work than others, which isn't fair. But, in the end, I think it's a good experience. I feel like I am learning to participate in a global workforce.

C. **Read each statement. Who expressed this idea? Write _J_ (Jin-soo) or _A_ (Adela). Write _B_ for both.**

_____ 1. I got used to working with others.

_____ 2. Students can explain things in a way that's easy to understand.

_____ 3. I learn about other points of view.

_____ 4. Group work can feel unfair.

_____ 5. It can be hard to find time to meet.

_____ 6. I am getting useful future work experience.

D. **Discuss these questions with a partner or in a small group.**

1. Do you like group work? Why or why not?

2. How often do you work in groups in class? Do you ever have to meet outside of class?

3. Describe a time when a classmate explained something in a way that was easy to understand.

4. How has collaborating helped you understand other people's points of view?

5. What is challenging about group work for you?

E. **The chart lists problems many students have with group work—and some solutions. Check (✓) the problems you have and the solutions you will try. Add your own ideas (problems and solutions you have experienced or have heard of). Share your ideas with your partner or group.**

Problem	Solution
☐ I find it awkward to work with people I don't know.	☐ Get to know the people in your group. Learning names can make group work easier.
☐ I never know what I'm supposed to do.	☐ Work together to decide everyone's responsibilities. Sometimes, everyone does the same work. Other times, the roles are different.
☐ I agreed to do something, but now I don't understand.	☐ Communicate with your group members. They can help you.
☐ I can't find time to meet the group.	☐ Collaborate using online tools. Everyone can work in the same document and make comments or chat.
☐ Something unexpected happened, and I can't meet.	☐ Let your group members know. Try to reschedule face-to-face meetings. They are valuable.
☐	☐
☐	☐
☐	☐

WHAT DID YOU LEARN?

Read the sentences. Check (✓) what you learned.

☐ I can follow a process.

☐ I can describe a process.

☐ I can use the comparative form of adjectives.

☐ I can build word families with prefixes.

☐ I can work in a group.

🔊 Go to **MyEnglishLab** to complete a self-assessment.

🔊 Go to **MyEnglishLab** for a challenge reading about Civil Engineering.

Unit 4 NATURAL SCIENCE

Sustainable Agriculture

Go to **MyEnglishLab** to watch an introduction about **NATURAL SCIENCE**.

Chapter 7 Feeding the World

CHAPTER PROFILE

Sustainable agriculture is an area of study that looks at raising food without harming the environment. In this chapter, you will study two popular forms of food production.

You will learn the answers to these questions:

- What is the difference between industrial agriculture and sustainable agriculture?

- What impact has industrial agriculture had on the world?

- What is agroecology, and how is it different from industrial agriculture?

OUTCOMES

- Identify comparison and contrast
- Make comparisons
- Use the superlative form of adjectives
- Use word maps
- Volunteer your time

For more about **SUSTAINABLE AGRICULTURE**, see Chapter 8. See also [OC] **SUSTAINABLE AGRICULTURE**, Chapters 7 and 8.

GETTING STARTED

Discuss these questions with a partner or in a small group.

1. Where do you get the food you eat? Do you grow your own, buy it at an outdoor market, go to a supermarket, or purchase it online? Which is best? Explain.

2. Is farming important in your culture? What crops (food) or livestock (animals) are raised? Do you think farming is an enjoyable profession? Explain.

3. Look at the pictures below. Each shows a different way of plowing—breaking up the ground so seeds can be planted. Describe each picture. What are the differences between the two practices? What are the similarities? Which are you more familiar with?

Plowing with a water buffalo

Plowing with a tractor

⬦ Go to **MyEnglishLab** to complete a self-assessment.

READ

SKILL: IDENTIFYING COMPARISON AND CONTRAST

WHY IT'S USEFUL By recognizing compare and contrast language and grammar structures, you can gain a deeper understanding of how things are similar or different.

Comparison is thinking about how ideas or things are similar (the same). **Contrast** is looking at how they are different. Writers use compare and contrast language and specific grammar when describing similarities and differences. Study the chart and examples.

COMPARE AND CONTRAST LANGUAGE		
When Comparing	**When Contrasting**	
both	but	on the other hand
like	different	unlike
similarly	however	while
too		

Horticulture—the study of plants—is a part of the agricultural science field. **Similarly,** animal science is a subject of the field.

I'm considering studying agricultural science. **On the other hand,** earth science really interests me, too.

Other Ways to Express Similarities and Differences

Writers also use the **comparative form of adjectives** to show the differences between two things.

> The field of horticulture is **older than** robotics. I think it's also **more interesting** because it involves studying living things.

Writers use the **superlative form of adjectives** to show how one thing has more of a particular quality than all other things.

> Some believe that neuroscience is **the hardest science field**. I agree but think ecology is **the most exciting**.

TIP

Good readers make comparisons between the information they read and information they already know. They ask themselves how the information is similar or different. This can deepen their understanding of the topic.

Try identifying the compare and contrast language.

- First, notice how the writer organized her ideas in a Venn diagram.
- Next, read the paragraph on the next page.
- Notice the boldfaced language the writer uses to explain similarities and differences.

Horticulture
- study of plants
- horticulturist
- works in parks, gardens, ag centers

ag science
- scientists
- work outside

Animal Science
- study of animals
- animal scientist
- works for industrialized farms

TIP

A Venn diagram is a kind of graphic organizer. It's good for classifying information into similarities and differences.

File　Home　Insert　Page layout　Object　Type　View　Window　Help

Horticulture and Animal Science

Horticulture and animal science are two areas of study with many similarities and differences. **Both** are subjects in ag science. In addition, **both** involve working outside with living things. **However**, horticulture looks at plant life, **while** animal science studies animal life. The scientists who work in these areas have **different** names: horticulturist and animal scientist. **While** they **both** work outside, they work in **different** areas.

REMEMBER

Circle <u>all</u> correct answers.

Use compare language to show _____ . Use contrast language to show _____ .

a. differences / similarities

b. relationship / effect

c. similarities / differences

d. importance / explanations

VOCABULARY PREVIEW

Read the words. Circle the ones you know. Put a question mark (?) next to the ones you don't know.

amount	consumer	fan (n)	produce (v)	reduce	season (n)

○ Go to **MyEnglishLab** to complete a vocabulary practice.

PREDICT

Preview the article "Food Production: Industrialized Versus Sustainable Agriculture" on the next page. Complete the tasks.

1. Look at the pictures. What are the similarities and differences between the two pictures of the chickens? What do you think the article will be about?

_____

2. Read the title and the first sentence of each paragraph. What is the main idea?
   a. People have many choices when buying food from supermarkets.
   b. Like sustainable agriculture, industrial agriculture is concerned about the environment.
   c. Industrial agriculture is different from sustainable agriculture because there is less concern about the environment.

READ

A. Read the article. Do not stop to look up words. Answer the questions.

Glossary

date (n): a small sweet brown fruit

habitat: the natural environment in which a plant or animal lives

industrialized (adj): having a lot of factories, mines, etc.

method: way of doing something

natural resources: things that exist in nature and can be used by people, for example, oil, trees, etc.

pesticide: a chemical substance used to kill insects and small animals that destroy crops

pollute: to make the air, water, or soil dirty by adding harmful substances

---

Food Production: Industrialized Versus Sustainable Agriculture

1 In industrialized countries, the supermarket is where most people buy their food. It's where, in any season, almost anything can be bought. Strawberries in winter? Of course. Fresh dates from Morocco? No problem. For today's shoppers, the supermarket is their oyster.

1. What tells you that two topics are being compared? Circle TWO answers.
   a. the title, including the word *versus*
   b. the first sentence of the paragraph
   c. the pictures showing two different ways of raising chickens
   d. the two different fruits mentioned in the paragraph

2. What two topics are being compared?
   a. food and farming
   b. industrialized farming and sustainable farming
   c. raising chickens and selling eggs
   d. supermarkets and food shops

2 [1]Who's responsible for this? [2]In two words: industrialized agriculture, also known as factory farming. [3]This is farming that uses machines to raise and produce animals and crops. [4]Since the early 20th century, factory farming has grown thanks to

Look at the Venn diagram the student used to organize her research. Then read her paragraph. Notice how she used the point-by-point pattern and comparison language.

Organic Food | Conventional Food

Organic Food
- is grown without chemicals
- is more expensive
- is more nutritious
- has more fatty acids and antioxidants

(overlap)
- is necessary for survival
- costs money
- is grown on farms and sold to consumers

Conventional Food
- is grown with chemicals
- is cheaper
- is less nutritious
- contains fewer fatty acids and antioxidants

| File | **Home** | Insert | Page layout | Object | Type | View | Window | Help |

Organic or Conventional?

Is organic food healthier than conventionally grown food? Organic food is food grown without the use of dangerous chemicals, **while** conventional food is produced with the help of chemical pesticides. **Unlike** a lot of conventional food, most organic food is expensive. **However**, recent research shows that organic food is also more nutritious. A study by the *British Journal of Nutrition* shows that organic dairy and meat contains more omega-3 fatty acids. These fatty acids can help reduce heart disease. **Similarly**, another study showed that organic crops also have more antioxidants, which help us fight off diseases. Some critics say that the amount of extra nutrients may be too small to make a big difference in our health, so it's not worth the extra money. **On the other hand**, supporters believe that the extra costs are well worth the added health benefits. In the end, consumers must make the choice for themselves.

REMEMBER

Circle the correct answer.

The point-by-point organizational pattern presents _____ , while the block pattern presents _____ .

a. two or more ideas in the same paragraph / each idea in a separate paragraph

b. each idea in a separate paragraph / two or more ideas in the same paragraph

Grammar for Writing Using the superlative form of adjectives

Use the **superlative form of the adjective** to compare three or more things. For example:

> The town has three supermarkets. Dilley's is the closest and the most expensive.

The number of syllables in an adjective decides its superlative form. Study the chart.

	Adjective	Superlative Form
One syllable Add *the* + *-est*.	large high cold	**the** larg**est** **the** high**est** **the** cold**est**
Two or more syllables Add *the most* + adjective.	common difficult important	**the most** common **the most** difficult **the most** important
When the adjective ends in *Y*, change *Y* to *i* and add *-est*.	easy	**the** easi**est**
Irregulars Some adjectives have irregular superlatives.	good bad far	the best the worst the farthest / the furthest
Use *one of / some of* + superlative form to describe a group or category of superlative things.	Farming is **one of the most difficult** jobs in the world. Farmers are **some of the busiest** people in the world.	

REMEMBER

Complete the sentence. Circle the correct answer.

The superlative form of adjectives is used to compare one thing to _____ .

a. a group of things   b. another thing

A. Read the paragraph. Underline the superlatives.

A Farming Life

Growing up in the country, most of our neighbors were dairy farmers. I saw how hard they worked and realized that farming is one of the most difficult jobs. Dairy cows need to be milked two to three times a day, so there is never a break. It is also difficult to take a vacation. In addition, farmers have to go to bed and get up the earliest of anyone I know. Most of our neighbors were up at 4 A.M. every day and in bed by 8 P.M. However, farmers are also some of the healthiest people I know. The time spent outdoors doing hard work keeps most of them in great shape. Farming is not the highest-paying job in the world, but it's one of the best because it helps to feed the world.

The opposite of *the most* is *the least*. The number of syllables is not important: *the least cold, the least common, the least difficult,* etc.

B. Complete the sentences. Use the superlative form of the boldfaced adjective.

1. Farmers are some of _____ (**busy**) people in the world.

2. Historians believe that one of _____ (**important**) steps in human development was when early humans learned how to raise plants and animals.

3. Instead of being nomadic—moving from place to place—these humans stayed in one place, which was _____ (**good**) way to grow food.

4. Archaeologists have found the remains of a 23,000-year-old hut (a simple, small house). Inside was _____ (**large**) collection of seeds from that time period.

5. This archaeological site is on the shore of Lake Kinneret. It was discovered in 1989 when the level of the lake was at _____ (**low**) level in years.

C. Compare and contrast dairy farmers with ranchers. Use the information in the Venn diagram and the words.

Dairy Farmers
- raise cows for milk
- must milk cows a few times a day
- cows kept in specific fields close to barns

(both)
- work with cows
- must feed, water, and care for cows
- use farm equipment like tractors
- have barns

Ranchers
- raise cows for meat
- cows may graze (eat over a lot of land)
- their farm is often called a ranch

1. (both) _____

_____

2. (like) _____

_____

3. (unlike) _____

_____

4. (while) _____

_____

⬥ Go to **MyEnglishLab** for more grammar practice.

WRITE A COMPARE / CONTRAST PARAGRAPH

STEP 1: READ TO WRITE

A. Preview the article. What is it about?

B. Read the article. Answer the questions.

> ### Glossary
>
> **antibiotic:** a drug that fights sickness in the body
>
> **dairy farm:** a farm that has cows and produces and sells milk
>
> **demand (n):** the need or desire that people have for goods and services
>
> **fertilizer:** a substance put on soil to help crops grow
>
> **harmful:** dangerous or causing damage
>
> **illness:** a disease of the body or mind
>
> **nutrient:** a chemical or food that provides what is needed for plants or animals to live and grow

Feeding the World or Harming It?

1 ¹In Brazil, the Bom Futuro Farm is the largest producer of soybeans in the world, producing 950,000 metric tons (1 million US tons) in 2017. ²Similarly, in China, the Mudanjiang City Mega Farm is the biggest dairy farm in the world, producing 800 million liters (211 million gal.) of milk each year. ³Their secret? ⁴Chemical fertilizers and antibiotics for animals.

 1. In Sentence 1 of Paragraph 1, the author is comparing the farm to _____ .
    a. all other vegetable producers
    b. all other soybean producers
    c. all other farms

2 ¹Since its introduction, chemical fertilizer has forever changed the way farmers grow crops. ²In the past, farmers planted a crop for a year or two but then waited until the nutrients returned before they reused that same land. ³With chemical fertilizer, which adds the nutrients back to the soil, farmers can plant the same crop in the same place year after year. ⁴This means large amounts of crops at the lowest costs in history.

 2. In Sentence 4, *lowest* describes the _____ .
    a. cost of fertilizers for farmers
    b. amount of crops produced
    c. cost of crops for farmers

3   In addition, farmers started giving antibiotics to animals to increase the animal's size and lifespan. Like with crops, this has meant some of the highest production rates and lowest costs in the history of farming.

3. The author uses *highest* and *lowest* to describe _____ . Circle TWO answers.
   a. crops
   b. rates
   c. costs

4   A win-win, right? Not everyone agrees. More food at a lower price sounds good, but many believe that these kinds of industrialized farming practices are more harmful than helpful. This fertilizer, for example, causes pollution and leads to global warming. In addition, planting the same crop year after year harms the soil. Also, large animal farms produce a lot of waste. This can make the water supply dangerous to drink. Critics also say the animals' living conditions are bad. Finally, some believe antibiotics can cause illness or even death in both animals and humans.

5   As the world population grows, the demand for food will, too. However, we must demand that food be grown safely.

4. The purpose of the article is to _____ .
   a. explain how industrialized farming is good for the world
   b. compare the best and worst parts of industrialized farming
   c. show why farmers must think about global warming

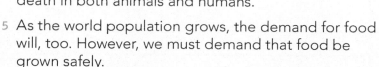

🔊 Go to **MyEnglishLab** to reread the article.

A dairy farm's robotic milking system

STEP 2: PREPARE TO WRITE

Think about eating in (cooking at home), eating out (at a restaurant), and getting take-out (food to-go). Prepare to write a compare / contrast paragraph (or two) about your experiences.

1. As you saw in Chapter 1, a **T-chart** is a graphic organizer that can help you categorize ideas. Study the example.

ORGANIC FOOD	CONVENTIONAL FOOD	HOME-GROWN FOOD
Pros		
• is healthy • is sometimes locally grown	• is inexpensive	
Cons		
• can be expensive	• may be grown with chemicals	

2. Brainstorm pros (good points) and cons (bad points) about each topic in the T-chart.

COOKING AT HOME	EATING OUT	GETTING TAKE-OUT
Pros		
Cons		

STEP 3: WRITE

Write your compare / contrast paragraph.

- Look at your T-chart as your write.

- Use compare and contrast language. Use point-by-point or block organization.

- Use superlatives. For example:

  Organic, conventional, and home-grown foods can all taste good. The most important thing is ...

STEP 4: PROOFREAD AND EDIT

A. Read your paragraph and circle any mistakes. Answer the questions in the chart.

Did you …	Yes	No	Notes
indent your paragraph?			
start each sentence with a capital letter?			
use correct punctuation to end each sentence?			
use clear organization?			
use compare and contrast language and clear organization?			
use superlatives?			

B. Share your paragraph with a partner. Read your partner's paragraph and answer the questions in the chart.

Peer Review Form	Notes
Where does the writer prefer to eat?	
How many sentences are there?	
Is there compare and contrast language? Are the ideas clearly organized?	
Did the writer use superlative adjectives?	
Is the paragraph formatted correctly? (indented with correct capitalization and punctuation)	
Do you have any questions or comments for the writer?	

C. Discuss the feedback with your partner. Ask questions about your partner's paragraph.

Why do you prefer eating out (or eating in)?

Is there ever a time when you prefer eating out?

How do you feel when you get take-out?

D. Discuss these questions with a partner or in a small group.

Which organizational pattern did you use? Why?

VOCABULARY STRATEGY

USING WORD MAPS

WHY IT'S USEFUL By using a word map, you can learn new information about a word.

Graphic organizers are a way to organize information visually. There are many graphic organizers that can help you learn new vocabulary. A **word map** is one example. A word map uses the definition as well as other information to help you learn new vocabulary. Study the chart and examples.

Information to Include	Other Information
• the word	• synonyms: words with a similar meaning
• the definition	• antonyms: words with a different meaning
• a picture	• the part of speech (noun, verb, adjective, adverb)
• a sentence with the word (taken from the reading)	• word family members: other form(s) of the word
	• association: what the reader thinks of when reading the word

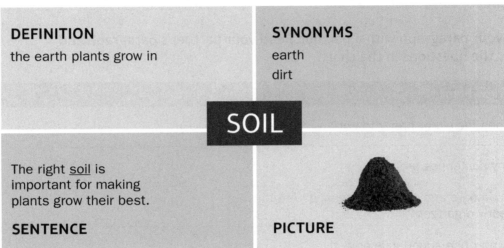

DEFINITION
the earth plants grow in

SYNONYMS
earth
dirt

SOIL

The right <u>soil</u> is important for making plants grow their best.

SENTENCE

PICTURE

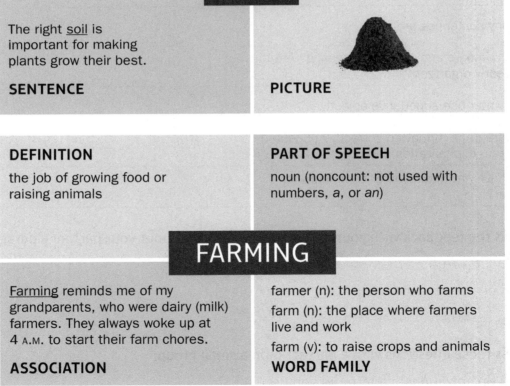

DEFINITION
the job of growing food or raising animals

PART OF SPEECH
noun (noncount: not used with numbers, *a*, or *an*)

FARMING

<u>Farming</u> reminds me of my grandparents, who were dairy (milk) farmers. They always woke up at 4 A.M. to start their farm chores.

ASSOCIATION

farmer (n): the person who farms
farm (n): the place where farmers live and work
farm (v): to raise crops and animals

WORD FAMILY

A. Read the excerpt from the upcoming reading, "Agroecology: The Solution to Food Production." Then complete the word map.

> While pesticides were used to control **insects**, now farmers use more natural, less harmful methods.

DEFINITION	SYNONYM(S)
	bug

INSECT

SENTENCE	PICTURE

B. Read two more excerpts from the upcoming reading, "Agroecology: The Solution to Food Production." Create your own word maps for *weed* and *survive*. Use a dictionary if necessary.

1. Some rice farmers keep ducks in their rice paddies, which eat the insects and **weeds** …

2. … this grain could **survive** drier, hotter conditions better than rice.

C. Choose three vocabulary words from "Food Production: Industrial Versus Sustainable Agriculture" on page 174 and create your own word maps. Then explain them to a partner.

1. Word: _____

2. Word: _____

3. Word: _____

D. Work with another student. Compare answers.

1. Do you have similar words for Part C? Are your word maps similar or different?

2. Do you think you will use word maps to learn new vocabulary? Why or why not?

APPLY YOUR SKILLS

In this chapter, you learned about the differences between industrial and sustainable farming. In Apply Your Skills, you will read about agroecology, which studies the impact of agriculture on the environment and people. You will also write a paragraph that compares farm life to city life.

BEFORE YOU READ

Discuss these questions with one or more students.

1. Ecology looks at the relationship between plants, animals, and people and their environment. Agriculture is the science of farming. How are these two sciences similar and different?

2. Rising sea level, global warming, and water and air pollution are examples of environmental problems that an ecologist might study. How can these problems affect farming? What can farmers do to help stop or slow these problems?

VOCABULARY PREVIEW
Read the words. Circle the ones you know. Put a question mark (?) next to the ones you don't know.

climate	condition (n)	depend on	gain (v)	goal	knowledge

◐ Go to **MyEnglishLab** to complete a vocabulary practice.

READ

A. Preview the article "Agroecology: The Solution to Food Production" on the next page. What is it about?

B. Read the article. Answer the questions.

> ### Glossary
> **a living:** the way you earn money
> **grain:** the seeds of a crop such as wheat, rice, or corn used as food
> **in response to:** as a reaction to
> **suicide:** the act of killing oneself

A farmer in a rice paddy field

Agroecology: The Solution to Food Production

1 In response to factory farming, a practice called *agroecology* has appeared. Agroecology uses local farming knowledge and practices and modern scientific technology to solve agricultural problems. Its goal is to work with local farmers and help them produce more food using sustainable methods. This new movement has gained support around the world, specifically in countries like India, where farming is common.

    1. The practice of _____ led to agroecology.
      a. agricultural problems
      b. local farming
      c. factory farming
      d. food production

2 In India, one-half of the country's 1.2 billion people depend on agriculture for a living. Most of the farms are small—only 3 acres. While industrial farming has benefitted some people, for many of these small farmers, it caused problems. Crops failed, and, in turn, the farmers didn't make much money. Meanwhile, many owed large amounts of money to banks or business owners or other people. This led to a large rate of suicide among farmers and food problems for many.

    2. Many small farmers in India _____ industrialized farming methods.
      a. had success with
      b. experienced problems because of
      c. depend on
      d. have benefitted from

(Continued)

3 However, thanks to more government support of sustainable methods, small farmers are starting to see their farms grow again. Instead of just planting one crop—like rice or corn—farmers are using crop rotation. For example, one season they plant rice, another season corn, another season wheat. This keeps the soil in the healthiest possible condition—full of nutrients, which results in more food.

Millet crop

4 Using fewer pesticides is another change. While farmers once used pesticides to kill insects, they now use more natural, less harmful methods. For instance, some rice farmers keep ducks in their rice paddies. The ducks eat the insects and weeds, and their waste acts as a natural fertilizer for the plants.

5 Finally, although much of India's diet is rice, some farmers know that other grains grow better in their area. Millet is a traditional grain of Tamil Nadu, an area of India, but many farmers weren't growing it. However, agroecological practices—which support traditional knowledge of the plants and climate—showed that this grain could survive better in hotter, drier conditions than rice could. Of all the grains, millet was the best grain for that area.

3. In Paragraphs 5, the author describes differences between _____ and rice.
   a. diet
   b. plants
   c. grain
   d. millet

6 While industrialized farming is still widely supported in most countries, the success of agroecology has shown the world that more natural methods can be highly successful.

4. The purpose of the article is to _____ .
   a. compare the farming practices in India with those in other countries
   b. explain how agroecology can lead to successful farming methods
   c. discuss the differences between industrialized farming and agroecology
   d. show why most countries use industrialized farming methods

C. Were your predictions in Before You Read correct?

🔊 Go to **MyEnglishLab** to reread the article.

B. Complete the word map. Then choose two words from any reading in this chapter and create a word map for each. Explain the words to a partner.

1.

DEFINITION	SYNONYM(S)
DRY	
SENTENCE	WORD FAMILY

2. Your word: _____ Reading title: _____

3. Your word: _____ Reading title: _____

◉ Go to **MyEnglishLab** to complete grammar and vocabulary practices.

ASSIGNMENT

In this chapter, you have read a lot about farming. Think about the differences between farm life and city life and write a comparison / contrast paragraph comparing the two.

PREPARE TO WRITE

A. Think about what you know about living on a farm (farm life) and living in a city (city life). Use the T-chart (or create a Venn diagram) to brainstorm pros and cons.

FARM LIFE	CITY LIFE
Pros	
Cons	

B. With a partner or in a small group, discuss your notes. Ask questions. For example:

What are the similarities between living in a city and living on a farm? What are the differences?

Which do you prefer? Why?

WRITE

Write a draft paragraph that compares farm life to city life.

- Use compare and contrast language. Use point-by-point or block organization.
- Use superlative adjectives.

PROOFREAD AND EDIT

A. Read your paragraph and circle any mistakes. Answer the questions in the chart.

Did you ...	Yes	No	Notes
indent your paragraph?			
start each sentence with a capital letter?			
use correct punctuation to end each sentence?			
compare city life to farm life?			
use compare and contrast language and clear organization?			
use superlatives?			

B. Share your paragraph with a partner. Read your partner's paragraph and answer the questions in the chart.

Peer Review Form	Notes
What is the paragraph about?	
How many sentences are there?	
Did the writer use comparison language? Are the ideas clearly organized?	
Are there some superlatives?	
Is the paragraph formatted correctly? (indented with correct capitalization and punctuation)	
Do you have any questions or comments for the writer?	

F. Discuss your feedback with a partner. Then write a second draft.

DEVELOP SOFT SKILLS

VOLUNTEERING YOUR TIME

Volunteering means doing work to help an individual or organization without pay. Many universities encourage students to volunteer while in school. Some universities even have a program that places students into volunteer positions. Volunteering is a good way to learn new skills and meet people. You can volunteer locally or go to another country. Projects range from volunteering in schools and hospitals, to serving meals to the homeless and cleaning up parks.

A. Preview the flyer. What is it about?

B. Read the flyer.

> Glossary
>
> host (n): the person who invites other people to his or her house
>
> room and board: a place to sleep and meals

CITY UNIVERSITY

Volunteer on an Organic Farm— Anywhere in the World

Summer break is just around the corner. It's a great time to help others by volunteering. If you are interested in sustainable agriculture and want to learn about organic farming practices, this is the volunteer opportunity for you!

CU's Agroecology Program and the organization Volunteers Worldwide (VW) have teamed up to offer an exciting volunteer opportunity to students interested in sustainable agriculture.

- Spend 1–4 weeks volunteering at an organic farm.
- Work 8 hours a day, 5 days a week.
- Enjoy free room and board. Live with a farm family or other volunteers.
- Stay local or go abroad! VW has host farms around the world.
- Name your interest. Volunteers are placed on farms that match their interest, from horticulture to animal care—and much more.

Volunteers return from their experience with a new and exciting understanding of organic farming practices. There are some things that can't be learned in a classroom!

Apply soon! Space is limited.

C. Read the flyer again. Then read each statement and circle *T* (true) or *F* (false). Correct the false statements.

T / F   1. Students at City University must volunteer to complete their degree.

T / F   2. VW helps students find summer jobs.

T / F   3. The flyer is focused on students who are interested in sustainable agriculture.

T / F   4. Organic farm volunteers need to travel to another country.

T / F   5. Volunteers may help an organic farmer take care of crops or animals.

T / F   6. Volunteers receive money for their work.

D. What are your interests? Do you like children? Animals? The outdoors? Make a list.

My Interests

_____   _____

_____   _____

_____   _____

_____   _____

_____   _____

E. Read the volunteer opportunities. Add other projects you know of. Check (✓) any that match your interests. Discuss your ideas with a partner.

Projects

- ☐ Building homes for low-income families
- ☐ Caring for animals at an animal shelter
- ☐ Having a conversation with seniors
- ☐ Picking up trash at a park or beach
- ☐ Planning after-school activities for teens
- ☐ Planting trees in a neighborhood
- ☐ Reading to children

- ☐ Serving meals to the homeless
- ☐ Taking care of a community garden
- ☐ Teaching a language to adults
- ☐ Visiting patients in a hospital
- ☐ _____
- ☐ _____

F. Choose three ideas from your list above. Then go online and find out more about volunteer opportunities at your school or in your area. Fill in the chart. Share your findings with a partner or a small group.

Type of Opportunity	Details

WHAT DID YOU LEARN?

Read the sentences. Check (✓) what you learned.

- ☐ I can identify comparison and contrast.
- ☐ I can make comparisons.
- ☐ I can use the superlative form of adjectives.
- ☐ I can use word maps.
- ☐ I can volunteer my time.

⬥ Go to **MyEnglishLab** to complete a self-assessment.

Chapter 8   The Future of Farming

CHAPTER PROFILE

In this chapter, you will learn how **sustainable agriculture** is using technology to meet the challenge of feeding the world.

You will learn the answers to these questions:

- How are technological advances changing the work of farmers?

- What is *biological control*, and how is it connected to sustainable agriculture?

- What are the challenges of feeding the world, and what can we do to meet them?

OUTCOMES

- Make inferences
- Support your ideas
- Use count and noncount nouns
- Create alphaboxes
- Solve problems

For more about **SUSTAINABLE AGRICULTURE**, see Chapter 7. See also [OC] **SUSTAINABLE AGRICULTURE**, Chapters 7 and 8.

GETTING STARTED

Discuss these questions with a partner or in a small group.

1. Many people use wearable technology—like fitness trackers or smart watches. What information do these devices give, and how can they be helpful? How could these devices be used with animals? Explain.

2. In the past, farmers have benefitted from technological advances. For example, the tractor made farming much easier. How do you think farmers are using new technologies—smartphones, tablets, robots, etc.—to make farming easier and better?

3. Look at the pictures and captions below. What challenges do farmers face? How do scientists and researchers play an important role in our food and its production?

A farmer showing crop damage caused by disease

A farmer looking at crop damage caused by drought (shortage of rain)

🔊 Go to **MyEnglishLab** to complete a self-assessment.

READ

SKILL: MAKING INFERENCES

WHY IT'S USEFUL By making inferences, you can understand information not found in the text.

When you read an article and understand an idea that is not actually written in the article, you are **inferencing**. An inference is a guess that is based on information from the text and your own thinking. When we read, we think about our own knowledge and experiences, and use that to help us to understand a text better.

Techniques for Inferencing

- As you read, ask **questions**, such as, "Why does the author include this detail?" and "What does the visual show?"

- Look for **textual clues** from the whole reading: title, text, visuals (diagrams and photos). What story is the author trying to tell?

- Use your **background knowledge.** Ask yourself, "What do I already know about this topic?" and "How does it connect to my reading?"

Try making inferences.

- First, read the questions below the article "Man and Machine."

- Next, read the article.

- Then try to answer the questions. What textual clues support your inference? Do you have helpful background knowledge?

- Read how another student answered. Do you agree?

> **Glossary**
>
> blacksmith: someone who makes tools out of iron

Man and Machine

On most American farms, you will find a John Deere® machine. Today, John Deere is an internationally known company, but in the early 19th century, it was just the name of a man. John Deere was born in 1804 in Vermont. Trained as a blacksmith, Deere had difficulty finding work in Vermont, so he moved to Illinois. The Illinois soil was different from Vermont's—harder to plow— so his plows would easily break. He experimented with designs until he had a new, improved plow. By 1857, he had started his company, and it was making more than 10,000 plows a year, as well as other farm tools. In 1858, Deere handed over the business to his son Charles, one of his nine children. From this modest beginning, the company has grown to be valued at more than $1 billion.

1. In what country was John Deere born?

   in the United States

   Textual clue: *Deere was born in Vermont, a state in the United States.*

2. Was Deere a creative man?

   Yes, he was an inventor who created a new plow design.

   Textual clue: *He experimented with designs.*

   Background knowledge: *In order to think of new designs and products, you must be creative.*

3. Is the John Deere company successful?

   yes

   Textual clue: *It's valued at more than $1 billion.*

REMEMBER

Circle <u>all</u> correct answers.

What information can help you make an inference?

a. visuals

b. your own experiences

c. questions

d. textual clues

VOCABULARY PREVIEW

Read the words. Circle the ones you know. Put a question mark (?) next to the ones you don't know.

behavior	care (n)	fitness	improve	result (n)	temperature

🔊 Go to **MyEnglishLab** to complete a vocabulary practice.

PREDICT

Preview the article "Smart Farms" on the next page. Complete the tasks.

1. Which ideas will be in the article? Circle Y (yes) or N (no).
   a. farm animals   Y / N
   b. farm machines / equipment Y / N
   c. how to cook dinner   Y / N

2. Read the title again and the first and last sentence of each paragraph. What is the main idea? Check (✓) your prediction.
   ☐ how to live on a farm
   ☐ how wearables are making animals smarter
   ☐ how technology is improving farming

READ

A. Read the article. Do not stop to look up words. As you answer the questions, underline the text that supports your answers.

> ### Glossary
>
> **biotechnology:** the use of living things such as cells and bacteria to make drugs, destroy waste, etc.
>
> **craze:** a fashion, game, type of music, etc., that is very popular for a short time
>
> **device:** a thing that you use for a particular purpose
>
> **efficient:** working well, quickly and without waste
>
> **get in on:** to participate
>
> **sample (n):** a small part of something that shows what the whole thing is like

Smart Farms

1   Farm animals are getting in on the wearable craze. Wearables—like fitness trackers—are appearing on cows, chickens, and pigs. These devices record things like the animal's temperature, movement, and behaviors (eating, sleeping). This information is sent to the farmer's computer and helps the farmer provide specialized care.

1. Why do the farmers put wearables on their animals?
   a. to be able to find the animals
   b. to allow the animals to sleep without interruption
   c. to track each animal's health

2. What helped you make that inference? Circle <u>all</u> correct answers.
   a. clues in the text
   b. the picture
   c. your background knowledge

2   Like smart homes, smart farms are becoming common. In addition to wearable technology, there are tractors that check the health of the soil, drones that decide if plants need water, and biotechnology that creates poisonous seeds to kill insects.

3. Which inferences can you make from Paragraph 2? Circle TWO answers.
   a. More farmers are using technology to manage the work on their farms.
   b. The technology sector is making products that can be used on farms.
   c. Plants need special fertilizer to help them grow.

3 Industrialized farms are not the only ones using this technology. Smaller farms are also benefitting. For example, in the Rift Valley in East Africa, a Dutch agricultural technology group is helping people study their soil. The company developed the technology when they saw that crops were not growing well. They believed that poor soil was the problem. Now, with a small device and a cellphone, farmers can take a sample of the soil, send the results to a database in the Netherlands, and within minutes, receive a report. The report tells them what nutrients need to be added to make the plants grow better.

4. Which inference can you make from Paragraph 3?
 a. Small farms do not have the money to use technology.
 b. The Dutch own many farms in East Africa.
 c. Poor soil can be improved.

4 Poor soil was also a problem for black bean farmers in Guatemala. Using biotechnology, scientists developed two new kinds of black bean seeds for the farmers. The seeds improve the soil quality and also fight off disease and pests.

5. Which inference can you make from Paragraph 4?
 a. The black bean farmers did not have a lot of money.
 b. Disease and pests are a problem for black bean farmers in Guatemala.
 c. The Guatemalan farmers were worried about the quality of their soil.

5 This marriage of technology with agriculture is making farming more efficient and productive. It's also improving the health of plants, animals, and farmers.

B. Were your predictions in Predict correct?

🔾 Go to **MyEnglishLab** to reread the article.

C. Reread the article. Then check (✓) the good inferences.

☐ 1. Farmers are benefitting from advances in technology.

☐ 2. Smart farm technology is often expensive.

☐ 3. In order to use this technology, some training is probably required.

☐ 4. The Dutch agricultural company has an office in the Netherlands.

☐ 5. The Guatemalan farmers had poor black bean crops in the past.

D. Read each statement and circle _T_ (true) or _F_ (false). Correct the false statements.

T / F   1. Wearable technology is used by people and animals.

T / F   2. Currently, only cows can use wearable technology.

T / F   3. Drones can be used to check on the health of plants.

T / F   4. The Rift Valley is in the Netherlands.

T / F   5. Biotechnology was used to make new black bean seeds.

T / F   6. Science and technology can help improve the lives of farmers.

E. Discuss these questions with a partner.

1. How has farm technology possibly affected your life? Explain.

2. How can information from wearables on animals help farmers?

3. Scientists have used biotechnology to create new seeds. Do you think food from these seeds is safe to eat? Explain.

F. We make inferences every day. For example, when we read a headline about a large earthquake, we infer that people died. Think of inferences you make while reading or in other situations.

VOCABULARY REVIEW
Complete the sentences. Use the words from the box. Use the correct form.

behavior	care	fitness	improve	result	temperature

1. Animal _____ is important to farmers. An animal that doesn't get enough exercise is probably going to have health problems.

2. Like in humans, in animals a high _____ can mean an illness and may require treatment.

3. When an animal is sick, its _____ changes. It may act tired and not eat.

4. After giving the sheep medicine, the vet saw positive _____ : They were eating and sleeping normally.

5. After the plants were given nutrients, they _____ : Their leaves became bigger and greener.

6. With plants, animals, and people, a little love and _____ can make a big difference.

↻ **Go to MyEnglishLab to read another article.**

WRITE

SKILL: SUPPORTING YOUR IDEAS

WHY IT'S USEFUL By including supporting sentences, you can help your reader understand your ideas and point of view.

Supporting your ideas is an important skill in academic life. For example, professors expect writing students to go beyond stating main ideas and opinions. They expect supporting details. When writing a paragraph in academic English, state your main idea in your topic sentence, which is usually the first sentence. This is followed by supporting sentences.

Supporting Sentences

Supporting sentences usually answer the questions of *who, what, when, where, why,* and *how.* They can include reasons, facts, examples, descriptions, and definitions.

The kind of supporting sentences you write depends on your writing goal.

- In an **opinion paragraph**, the supporting sentences may include facts, reasons, and examples. They may also try to persuade.

- In a **description paragraph**, the supporting sentences should include *sensory details*. These help the reader to see, hear, feel, taste, and touch the things you are describing.

- In a **narrative paragraph**, which is a real-life story, the supporting sentences should be structured to create a beginning, middle, and end.

- In a **research paper** (also called an *expository essay*), the supporting sentences may include facts gathered from research, definitions, and examples.

Read the student notes to see the topic sentences and support she is considering. Then read her paragraph on the next page to see which topic she chose. Notice how she supports her main idea with facts, examples, and opinions.

NOTES

IDEA #1

Topic sentence: The life of the inventor, John Deere, is very interesting.

Facts: information about John Deere's life

Reasons: why John Deere's life is very interesting

IDEA #2

Topic sentence: Growing a garden involves more than luck—it takes a lot of knowledge.

Facts: what you need to know before you plant a garden, or where to get knowledge about gardening (people, books, Internet)

Reasons: why knowledge is more important than luck

Example: a success story about gardening

My First Year Gardening

Topic sentence

¹ Growing a garden involves more than luck—it takes a lot of knowledge. ² When I bought my first house, I was excited to grow my own food, but my first year was a disaster. ³ Weeds were the only thing that did well. ⁴ I realized that I knew nothing about growing a garden, but I wanted to learn. ⁵ The first thing I did was talk to experts. ⁶ I spoke with people at the local garden center. ⁷ They told me what grew well in my area. ⁸ They also told me to test the soil, which I did. ⁹ I discovered that I needed to add nutrients, like nitrogen, to my soil. ¹⁰ They also suggested some books, which gave me information about how to feed and water my plants. ¹¹ According to these books, I wasn't giving my plants enough water, so I changed my watering habits. ¹² These changes led to amazing results. ¹³ This year, my vegetables are beautiful. ¹⁴ Some people might say I have a green thumb. ¹⁵ But that suggests I was born with a natural ability to grow plants. ¹⁶ In my opinion and experience, knowledge from expert advice is what helped my plants grow!

Narrative

Fact

Opinion

REMEMBER

Circle all correct answers.

Supporting sentences can be _____ .

a. facts   b. examples   c. descriptions   d. definitions

Grammar for Writing **Using count and noncount nouns**

Most nouns can be classified into two groups: **count and noncount nouns**.

Any noun that can be counted is a count noun. For example:

one cow → two cows   one sheep → two sheep

Nouns that cannot be counted are noncount nouns. These nouns are always treated as one quantity or group. For example:

water   sugar   money

In order to count noncount nouns, you must use a **quantifier** (a word or phrase that signals an amount or quantity).

a glass of water   a little sugar   some money

Quantifiers explain how many or how much. They are used with both count and noncount nouns. Note that *some* and *a lot of* can be used with both count and noncount nouns.

Study the chart.

QUANTIFIERS	
Used with Count Nouns	
Singular *a, an* (indefinite articles) *every, each*	Dairy farmers need **a barn** to house their cows. If **every farmer** used sustainable farming practices, our world would be much healthier.
Plural *many* *a few* *a lot of* *some*	During the harvest, the farmer employed **many workers**. My lemon tree produced **a few lemons** this year. The farmer had **a lot of tractors**. **Some workers** left when winter came.
Used with Noncount Nouns	
a little *much* (usually negative) *a lot of* *some*	I do **a little work** in the garden each morning. We did not get **much rain**. There was **a lot of farm equipment** in the barn. I ate **some fruit** for breakfast.

GRAMMAR NOTE

Count nouns have a singular and plural form (*barn, barns*), but noncount nouns have only one form: singular (*equipment*).

REMEMBER

Complete the sentence. Circle the correct answer.

Words that are used to count both count and noncount nouns are called _____ .

a. singular   b. plural   c. quantifiers   d. amounts

A. Reach each sentence. Then identify each boldfaced word as *C* (count) or
   N (noncount).

_____ 1. **Insects** are very important in keeping our world healthy.

_____ 2. For example, the honeybee does much more than produce **honey**.

_____ 3. In order to make honey, the honeybee must go from **flower** to flower to collect
nectar—a sweet liquid.

_____ 4. As they collect nectar, they also get a little **pollen** from the flower.

_____ 5. When they go to another flower, this pollen may get on another flower. This
is called *pollination*. Pollination is needed for a plant to develop fruit, which
contains **seeds**.

B. Complete the sentences with the quantifiers from the box. More than one correct answer may be possible.

a few	a little	a lot of	many	some

1. In order to have a profitable dairy farm, you need to have _____ cows.

2. It takes _____ work to run a dairy farm because cows must be milked a few times a day.

3. If you have only one cow, you will produce only _____ milk.

4. When working with cows, there are _____ rules to remember. For example, don't surprise a cow. She may kick and hurt you.

5. Working with animals takes _____ patience and hard work.

C. Read each topic sentence. Then write ideas for supporting sentences.

1. Farm technologies have improved farmers' lives.

Fact(s): _____

Reason(s): _____

Description(s): _____

Example(s): _____

2. Topic sentence: Agricultural science is more interesting than chemical engineering.

Fact(s): _____

Reason(s): _____

Description(s): _____

Example(s): _____

3. Topic sentence: The fast-food industry has benefitted from industrialized farming.

Fact(s): _____

Description(s): _____

Definition(s): _____

Example(s): _____

○ Go to **MyEnglishLab** for more grammar practice.

WRITE A PARAGRAPH WITH SUPPORTING SENTENCES

STEP 1: READ TO WRITE

A. Preview the article. What is it about?

B. Read the article. Answer the questions.

Glossary

allergic: likely to get sick if you eat, touch, or breathe a particular thing

control (v): to make someone or something do what you want

destroy: to break or damage something completely

eat into: to gradually reduce the amount of time, money, etc., that is available

effective: getting the result you want

enemy: a person or country that is not friendly to you and wants to harm or fight you

predator: an animal that kills and eats other animals

unusual: not normal; strange

Insects: A Farmer's Friend

1 [1]In the 1960s, Jan Koppert was a cucumber farmer in the Netherlands. [2]Pests were eating his plants. [3]So like most farmers, Koppert used chemical pesticides to control them. [4]However, when he became allergic to the pesticides, he realized he needed something else. [5]He discovered that the pests that were eating his cucumbers had a natural enemy: the predatory mite. [6]Soon his cucumbers were safe again.

    1. Are the nouns in Sentence 5 count or noncount? _____

2 [1]Koppert's story isn't unusual. [2]Pests have always been a big problem for farmers, destroying crops and eating into profits. [3]In turn, farmers have searched for a solution. [4]When chemical pesticides arrived in the early 20th century, many people thought they were the answer. [5]But that belief has changed in recent years. [6]While chemical pesticides are great at killing pests, they can also kill other plants, pollute groundwater, and harm animals and farmworkers.

    2. What is the noncount noun in Sentence 6? _____

(Continued)

3 ¹Biological control (using a pest's natural enemy like Koppert did) has none of those problems. ²And although chemical pesticides kill pests faster, biological controls are usually less expensive and more effective over time. ³As a result, today, many farms interested in sustainable farming methods use biological control. ⁴For example, in South America, the sugarcane borer destroys sugarcane crops and eats a lot of the corn and rice. ⁵Its enemy is a wasp that eats the borer when it is still a caterpillar. ⁶When researchers realized this, they started to use the wasps to control the borer.

3. What quantifiers appear in Paragraph 3? _____

4 ¹Biological control has become so popular that many farmers now buy natural predators like these online. ²One such company is Koppert Biological Systems, started by cucumber farmer Jan Koppert after his mite discovery. ³Today, Koppert sells his natural pest control products in 96 countries.

4. What does the quantifier in Sentence 1 tell you?

_____

5 ¹To sustainable farmers, the answer to pests is clear. ²From ladybugs eating aphids or wasps dining on moths, insects can be very valuable friends.

Aphids and whiteflies are a common pest for many agricultural farms. These very small insects feed on the plant and damage it. But they have many natural enemies, including ladybugs, who eat the pests.

◐ Go to **MyEnglishLab** to reread the article.

STEP 2: PREPARE TO WRITE

Jan Koppert's life changed when he discovered he was allergic to pesticides. From this discovery, his company was born. Prepare to write about an important experience that changed your life, using supporting sentences.

1. As you saw in Chapter 6, a **Q&A chart** is a graphic organizer that can help you brainstorm ideas by using questions and answers. Study the example.

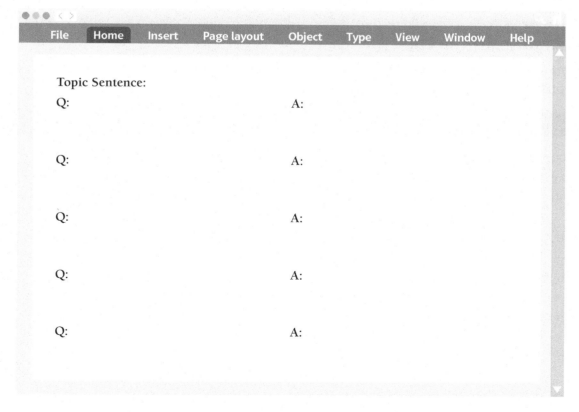

| File | Home | Insert | Page layout | Object | Type | View | Window | Help |

Topic Sentence: The day I moved to the United States was the most memorable day of my life.

Q: What happened on this day?

A: I left my family to study at a university in the US.

Q: Why was it memorable?

A: It was the first time I had traveled by myself.

Q: How old was I?

A: I was 18.

Q: Where was I living before moving to the US?

A: I was living in Istanbul, Turkey.

Q: How did I feel when I left my home country?

A: I was a little nervous but also excited for the adventure.

2. Decide which experience you will write about. Then write your topic sentence and brainstorm five questions and answers about your main idea. Try to include in your answers facts, reasons for your opinions, descriptions, and / or examples.

| File | Home | Insert | Page layout | Object | Type | View | Window | Help |

Topic Sentence:

Q: **A:**

Q: **A:**

Q: **A:**

Q: **A:**

Q: **A:**

STEP 3: WRITE

Write your paragraph with supporting sentences.

- Look at your Q&A chart as you write.

- Use supporting sentences to explain the reasons why this event is important or memorable.

- Use count and noncount nouns and quantifiers. For example:

  The day I moved to the United States is the most memorable day of my life. I was only 18 and didn't have much experience traveling alone.

STEP 4: PROOFREAD AND EDIT

A. Read your paragraph and circle any mistakes that you see. Answer the questions in the chart.

Did you …	Yes	No	Notes
indent your paragraph?			
start each sentence with a capital letter?			
use correct punctuation to end each sentence?			
write about a personal event?			
use supporting sentences?			
use count / noncount nouns and quantifiers?			

B. Share your paragraph with a partner. Read your partner's paragraph and answer the questions in the chart.

Peer Review Form	Notes
What is the paragraph about?	
How many sentences are there?	
Did the writer explain a personal event?	
Did the writer use supporting sentences to explain the importance of the event?	
Did the writer use count / noncount nouns and quantifiers?	
Is the paragraph formatted correctly? (indented with correct capitalization and punctuation)	
Do you have any questions or comments for the writer?	

C. Discuss the feedback with your partner. Ask questions about your partner's paragraph.

How did that event change your life?

Do you wish that event had never happened?

Did that event change anybody else's life?

D. Discuss these questions with a partner or in a small group.

Do you think a writer can give too much information (have too many supporting sentences)? Can too much support be bad? Explain.

VOCABULARY STRATEGY

CREATING ALPHABOXES

WHY IT'S USEFUL By using an alphabox, you can see all of the vocabulary words you have learned "at a glance."

Alphaboxes are a kind of graphic organizer. They are similar to a word wall where you record all the words you know about a certain topic. You fill in the boxes with the vocabulary starting with the letter for that box.

For example, *tractor* would go in the *T* box. As time goes on, you add to the boxes. Alphaboxes help remind you of the words you have learned. However, if you need more specific information (definitions, synonyms, parts of speech), you will need to use another graphic organizer.

A. **Read this excerpt from "Food for All" on page 216. Then add to the alphabox farming and food words.**

> The island of Singapore is mostly urban, with only about 250 acres of land used for agriculture. Because there is so little farmland, most of the island's food must be shipped in from other countries. But Jack Ng had a different idea. His Sky Greens company grows cabbage, lettuce, and other green vegetables in vertical greenhouses. Go into one of his greenhouses and you'll see rows of plants placed on A-shaped towers. Each tower has about 22 to 26 rows, which turn slowly—like a wheel—to reach the natural sunlight. Since these plants are indoors, there's less need for pesticides, and less use of land and water. However, more vegetables are grown.

A acres, agriculture	B	C	D
E	F	G grow	H
I	J	K	L
M	N	O	P pesticides
Q	R	S	T
U	V	W water	XYZ

B. **Add to your alphabox any vocabulary you have learned that is about farming. Then choose three of those terms and explain them to a partner.**

C. **Take one of the words from your alphabox and create a word map. Then share it with a partner.**

D. **Discuss these questions with one or more students.**

1. Do you have similar vocabulary written in your alphaboxes? Add new words if needed.

2. What strategies do you already use to learn new vocabulary? Do you think you will use alphaboxes or word maps to help you remember new vocabulary? Explain.

APPLY YOUR SKILLS

In this chapter, you learned how new technology and ideas are changing traditional farming practices. In Apply Your Skills, you will read how researchers and farmers are planning to meet the growing, global demand for food. You will also write a paragraph about a typical dish (prepared food) from your country.

BEFORE YOU READ

Discuss these questions with one or more students.

1. Currently, the world's population is a little over 7 billion people. This number is expected to grow to almost 10 billion by 2050. What challenges could this growth cause?

2. Experiential learning is when students learn through experience. For example, students may learn about dairy cows by taking a field trip or doing an internship at a dairy farm. What are the benefits of this type of education?

VOCABULARY PREVIEW

Read the words. Circle the ones you know. Put a question mark (?) next to the ones you don't know.

as long as	disagree	earn	increase (v)	indoors	row (n)

⬆ Go to **MyEnglishLab** to complete a vocabulary practice.

READ

A. Preview the article "Food for All" on the next page. What is it about?

B. Read the article. Answer the questions.

Glossary

consider: to think about something
entrepreneur: someone who starts a new business or arranges business deals in order to make money
exporter: a person or firm involved in selling goods abroad
graduate student: someone who is studying at a university to get a master's degree or PhD
irrigation: the act of making water flow to dry lands or crops
urban: relating to a town or city
vertical: pointing straight up

Food for All

1 The island of Singapore is mostly urban, with only about 250 acres of land used for agriculture. Because there is so little farmland, most of the island's food must be shipped in from other countries. But Jack Ng had a different idea. His company Sky Greens grows cabbage, lettuce, and other green vegetables in vertical greenhouses. Go into one of his greenhouses and you'll see rows of plants placed on A-shaped towers. Each tower

Plants in a vertical greenhouse

has about 22 to 26 rows, which turn slowly—like a wheel—to reach the natural sunlight. Since these plants are indoors, there's less need for pesticides and less use of land and water. However, more vegetables are grown.

1. What can you infer from Paragraph 1? Circle TWO answers.
   a. In the future, Jack Ng's greenhouses will make enough food to feed everyone in Singapore.
   b. Food is probably expensive in Singapore.
   c. Jack Ng has plans to open animal farms.
   d. Singapore is surrounded by water.

2 Using less to grow more is what the Food and Agricultural Organization (FAO) of the United Nations wants the world to do. By 2050, the world population will reach 10 billion, according to the UN. That's almost 3 billion more people on Earth than we have today. As long as the population increases, more people will move to urban areas and earn more money. There will be a bigger demand for water and food—especially meat, vegetables, and fruit, which people eat more of when they have more money. Many worry that there won't be enough food for everyone. But agricultural experts disagree. They think there will be enough—if agricultural methods change.

2. What can you infer from Paragraph 2? Circle TWO answers.
   a. The FAO is concerned about meeting the world's food demands.
   b. The 3 billion new people will mostly be poor.
   c. Urban areas have more job opportunities (with better pay) for people.
   d. People will eat less meat in the future.

3 ¹Like the FAO, researchers from Wageningen University and Research (WUR) in the Netherlands are leading the way. ²WUR is one of the world's best agricultural universities, and its professors work closely with entrepreneurs like Jack Ng to fix food problems. ³Consider how great the Dutch are at growing food. ⁴The Netherlands is small and only 1,000 miles from the Arctic Circle. ⁵However, the Dutch are one of the world's biggest exporters of potatoes, onions, and tomatoes. ⁶They, like Jack Ng, use greenhouses and other creative farming methods. ⁷For example, LED lighting is used so plants can grow 24 hours a day. ⁸Another method is hydroponic farming—the growing of plants in nutrient-rich water, not soil. ⁹Sustainable farming methods like rainwater irrigation, biological control, and natural fertilizer are also used.

Irrigation

¹⁰In addition, WUR has graduate students from more than 45 countries. Many students are working on sustainable agricultural projects in their home countries.

3. Which sentence supports the inference that the Dutch climate can be cold?
   a. Sentence 4
   b. Sentence 5
   c. Sentence 9
   d. Sentence 10

4 Like FAO and WUR, supporters of sustainable agriculture around the world are hopeful about the future of food. They believe that if every country uses these new methods, there will be enough food for all, for many years to come.

C. Were your predictions in Before You Read correct?

◐ Go to **MyEnglishLab** to reread the article.

D. Reread the article. Circle the correct answers.

1. Jack Ng is an example of a(n) _____ .

   a. leader

   b. farmer

   c. entrepreneur

   d. gardener

2. Using vertical greenhouses instead of horizontal ones is good when land is _____ .

    a. limited

    b. cheap

    c. polluted

    d. plentiful

3. People eat more meat, vegetables, and fruit when they have _____ .

    a. a lot of time to cook

    b. a few children

    c. more money

    d. many health problems

4. The author uses the example of food production in the Netherlands to show how people are _____ .

    a. creating solutions to food problems

    b. learning about global food production

    c. using industrial farming methods

    d. studying agroecology

5. The purpose of the article is to _____ .

    a. discuss the United Nations' work with food production

    b. show the importance of working independently

    c. explain how research and new farming methods can help meet future food demand

    d. compare and contrast the farming methods used in the Netherlands and Singapore

E. Complete the tasks. Discuss your ideas with a partner.

1. What can a good reader do to make inferences? Circle TWO answers.
    a. think about what he or she already knows about the topic
    b. look in a dictionary
    c. ask questions
    d. make sure he or she understands every word of the text

2. When writing about a topic, it's important to give support (reasons, facts, descriptions, examples, definitions). How does the author of "Food for All" support the idea that the world is working on meeting future food demands?

    _____

    _____

VOCABULARY REVIEW

Read each sentence. Then write the correct meaning of the boldfaced word. Use the definitions from the box.

becomes more in amount or number	inside a building
get money for work	lines of things
have a different opinion	with the condition that

1. Because farmers usually do not **earn** a lot of money for their work, many younger people are not interested in the farming profession.

   Definition: _____

2. Greenhouses, where plants are grown **indoors**, are popular for farmers who want to plant year-round but can't because of the climate.

   Definition: _____

3. In a vertical greenhouse, plants are arranged in **rows** that are stacked on top of each other. In a traditional greenhouse, plants grow next to each other.

   Definition: _____

4. Some believe that the world can meet future food demands. But others **disagree**, pointing out that today more than 800 million people in the world suffer from hunger.

   Definition: _____

5. Hopefully, as the number of farmers practicing sustainable farming **increases**, the number of hungry people will decrease.

   Definition: _____

6. **As long as** the world population continues to grow, land values will continue to increase.

   Definition: _____

THINK CRITICALLY

The article "Food for All" explains how universities, like WUR, have graduate students from around the world working on food projects. Use information from the article to answer the questions. Then discuss your ideas with a partner.

1. Why is having graduate students from around the world working on food projects good for global food production?

   _____

   _____

2. How might these students change their home country's farming methods?

   _____

   _____

3. How can having more diversity (students from different countries) improve student learning?

_____

_____

THINK VISUALLY

Vegetables provide many nutrients (vitamins A and C, etc.) that are important to people's health. The charts show global production of vegetables in 2016. Use information from the charts to answer the questions. Then discuss your ideas with a partner.

Top 10 World Producers of Corn, Potatoes, and Tomatoes, 2016 (in metric tons)

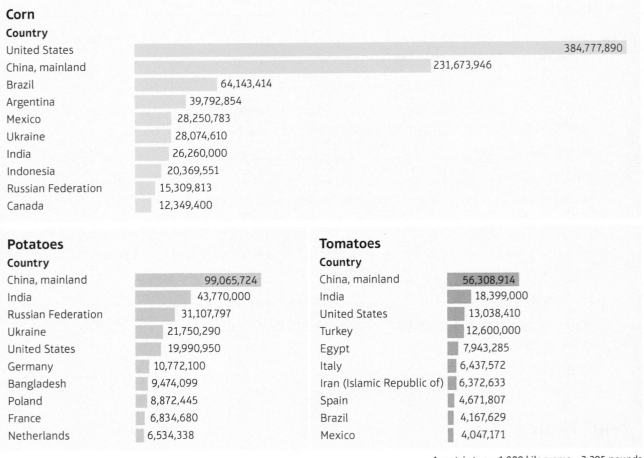

Corn

Country	
United States	384,777,890
China, mainland	231,673,946
Brazil	64,143,414
Argentina	39,792,854
Mexico	28,250,783
Ukraine	28,074,610
India	26,260,000
Indonesia	20,369,551
Russian Federation	15,309,813
Canada	12,349,400

Potatoes

Country	
China, mainland	99,065,724
India	43,770,000
Russian Federation	31,107,797
Ukraine	21,750,290
United States	19,990,950
Germany	10,772,100
Bangladesh	9,474,099
Poland	8,872,445
France	6,834,680
Netherlands	6,534,338

Tomatoes

Country	
China, mainland	56,308,914
India	18,399,000
United States	13,038,410
Turkey	12,600,000
Egypt	7,943,285
Italy	6,437,572
Iran (Islamic Republic of)	6,372,633
Spain	4,671,807
Brazil	4,167,629
Mexico	4,047,171

1 metric ton = 1,000 kilograms = 2,205 pounds

1. Which country produced the most corn? Potatoes? Tomatoes? How much?

_____

2. Which vegetable has the highest rate of production? What are some possible reasons for that?

_____

3. Are any of these vegetables common in your home country's traditional dishes? What vegetables does your country produce a lot of?

_____

_____

THINK ABOUT LANGUAGE

A. Fill in the chart with the words from the box. Classify the nouns as count or noncount nouns.

| agriculture | demand | hour | meat | school | vegetable |
| country | greenhouse | land | problem | sunlight | water |

Count Nouns	Noncount Nouns

B. Circle the correct quantifiers to complete each sentence.

1. Most farmers in the world have only **a little / a few** land to plant their crops.

2. In my family, we eat a lot of eggs but **not much / many** meat.

3. In countries without **much / many** hours of sunlight, some farmers use LED lighting and greenhouses.

4. Nowadays, there are not **much / many** schools that teach traditional ways of farming.

5. Planting one crop, year after year, can cause **much / many** problems in the soil.

6. Not **much / many** water is needed to grow prickly pears.

C. Read this excerpt from "Food for All." Add to your alphabox any food or farming vocabulary. Then discuss the words with a partner.

Hydroponic farming

Like the FAO, researchers from Wageningen University and Research (WUR) in the Netherlands are leading the way. WUR is one of the world's best agricultural universities, and its professors work closely with entrepreneurs to fix food problems. Consider how great the Dutch are at growing food. Although it is small and only 1,000 miles from the Arctic Circle, the Netherlands is one of the world's biggest exporters of potatoes, onions, and tomatoes. They, like Jack Ng, use greenhouses and other creative farming methods. For example, LED lighting is used so plants can grow 24 hours a day. Another method is hydroponic farming—the growing of plants in nutrient-rich water, not soil. Sustainable farming methods like rainwater irrigation, biological control, and natural fertilizer are also used. In addition, WUR has graduate students from more than 45 countries, and many are working on sustainable agricultural projects in their home countries.

🔊 **Go to MyEnglishLab to complete grammar and vocabulary practices.**

ASSIGNMENT

Think about what you have read about food production. Write a paragraph about a typical dish (a prepared food) from your culture, supporting it with details.

PREPARE TO WRITE

A. Think about the chart "Top 10 World Producers of Corn, Potatoes, and Tomatoes" on page 220. Think about your own experience eating a popular, local food. Brainstorm questions about your topic or use the questions from the box, and then answer them.

What is a traditional dish eaten in my country?	Why …
How is it made?	Who …
Is it eaten on special occasions or every day?	Where …

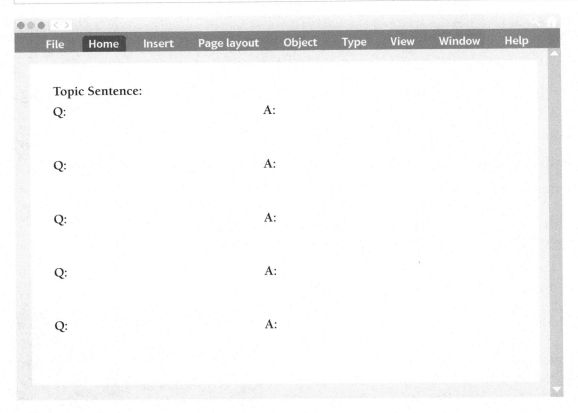

B. With a partner or in a small group, discuss your notes. Ask questions. For example:

Who usually prepares the food?

Who eats the food (rich / poor, young / old)?

Where is it served (homes, restaurants, schools)?

WRITE

Write a draft paragraph that explains your topic.

- Describe the dish using supporting sentences.
- Use count and noncount nouns with quantifiers.

PROOFREAD AND EDIT

A. Read your paragraph and circle any mistakes. Answer the questions in the chart.

Did you ...	Yes	No	Notes
indent your paragraph?			
start each sentence with a capital letter?			
use correct punctuation to end each sentence?			
describe a typical dish from your country?			
give support? (facts, reasons, descriptions, examples)			
use count / noncount nouns and quantifiers?			

B. Share your paragraph with a partner. Read your partner's paragraph and answer the questions in the chart.

Peer Review Form	Notes
What is the paragraph about?	
How many sentences are there?	
Did the writer give support? (descriptions, details, examples)	
Are there some count / noncount nouns and quantifiers?	
Is the paragraph formatted correctly? (indented with correct capitalization and punctuation)	
Do you have any questions or comments for the writer?	

C. Discuss your feedback with a partner. Then write a second draft.

● Go to **MyEnglishLab** to read another article.

DEVELOP SOFT SKILLS

SOLVING PROBLEMS

Being able to **solve problems** is an important skill for university success. There will be many times when you face a problem and need to think of a solution in order to move forward and achieve your goals.

A. Preview the conversation. What is it about?

B. Read the conversation.

XIU YING: Hi Aroon, how's your Friday going?

AROON: Mostly fine, but I have a problem.

XIU YING: Oh yeah. What's up?

AROON: Well, I have to write a ten-page paper. It's due Monday, but I also have an exam Monday and need to study.

XIU YING: So the problem is that you have too much work and too little time?

AROON: Yes, exactly.

XIU YING: OK, let's brainstorm some ideas. Can you ask for extra time to write the paper? Or get help from the Writing Center? What about talking to a librarian to help with your research?

AROON: Whoa, that's a lot of ideas. The professor does give extra time—I can send her an email.

XIU YING: Good. Now the exam. Have you thought about joining a study group? Can you sign up for an exam preparation session? Have you looked at practice exams?

AROON: These are all good ideas. I'll look at the professor's website and see if I can find some practice exams.

XIU YING: Sounds good. Do you feel a little better?

AROON: Yes. Thanks. Oh! I have to go. I have soccer practice.

XIU YING: Wait. What about the paper and studying?

AROON: Huh? But I love soccer.

XIU YING: Aroon, you need to focus on your studies. What other activities can you cancel this weekend?

AROON: Well, soccer, and I was planning to see a movie with my partner. … I guess I can cancel the movie.

XIU YING: See? Now you have more time. Let me know which ideas work for you.

AROON: OK. Thanks Xiu Ying!

C. Read the webpage. Then write the parts of the conversation that match the steps.

Step 1: _____

Step 2: _____

Step 3: _____

Steps to Successful Problem-Solving

Have a problem that you can't solve? Follow these steps for successful problem-solving:

Step **1** What is the problem? Write it down or define it in some way.

Step **2** What is the cause of the problem? Try to understand what is creating the problem.

Step **3** What are possible solutions? Brainstorm a list of possible solutions.

Step **4** Which is the best solution? Choose one and try it.

Step **5** Is it working? If yes, great. If not, try another one.

D. Discuss the question with a partner or in a small group.

What are other possible solutions to Aroon's problem?

E. Think of a problem that you need help with. What is the problem? What is the cause? What are the possible solutions? Which is the best solution? Share your ideas with a partner.

1. What is the problem? _____

2. What is the cause? _____

3. What are possible solutions? _____

4. Which is the best solution? _____

WHAT DID YOU LEARN?

Read the sentences. Check (✓) what you learned.

☐ I can make inferences.

☐ I can support my ideas.

☐ I can use count and noncount nouns.

☐ I can create alphaboxes.

☐ I can solve problems.

🔊 Go to **MyEnglishLab** to complete a self-assessment.

🔊 Go to **MyEnglishLab** for a challenge reading about Sustainable Agriculture.

Index

Photo Credits